"Whoever Whitley Strieber's strange visitor was in the small hours of June 6, 1998, he delivered a Hall of Records full of wisdom, hope, and enlightenment for mankind. What we're doing here on this planet, in these lives, is part of a much larger process, the secret outlines of which we can barely even glimpse. *The Key* is the latest and perhaps the most accessible installment of the perennial philosophy that wise teachers have gifted to mankind these past ten thousand years to help us find our way to the truth. Read it, take time to reflect, consider its messages, and you'll find it has worked a kind of magic on you."

—GRAHAM HANCOCK, AUTHOR OF
FINGERPRINTS OF THE GODS

"For over two decades now, Whitley Strieber has been producing an exceptionally nuanced, and exceptionally eerie, body of work that is designed to shock us out of our dualistic ways of thinking and being around religion, science, and soul. Whatever its source, *The Key* is easily one of the most concise and provocative texts within this corpus and the larger American metaphysical tradition that it both channels and, in the process, transforms."

—JEFFREY J. KRIPAL, CHAIR OF THE DEPARTMENT OF
RELIGIOUS STUDIES AT RICE UNIVERSITY AND
AUTHOR OF *AUTHORS OF THE IMPOSSIBLE:
THE PARANORMAL AND THE SACRED*

the KEY

A TRUE ENCOUNTER

Whitley Strieber

A TARCHERPERIGEE BOOK

an imprint of Penguin Random House LLC
penguinrandomhouse.com

Most TarcherPerigee books are available at special quantity discounts for bulk
purchase for sales promotions, premiums, fund-raising, and educational needs.
Special books or book excerpts also can be created to fit specific needs.
For details, write SpecialMarkets@penguinrandomhouse.com

Library of Congress Cataloging-in-Publication Data

Strieber, Whitley.
The key: a true encounter/Whitley Strieber.
p.   cm.
ISBN 978-1-58542-869-4
1. Spiritual life—Miscellanea.   2. Strieber, Whitley.   I. Title.
BF1999.S82   2011   2011003198
001.94—dc22

Printed in the United States of America

BOOK DESIGN BY NICOLE LAROCHE

This book is dedicated to Anne Strieber.

Without her insistence, it would have been

neither written nor published.

CONTENTS

the KEY

MEETING *the* MASTER *of the* KEY

I did not know it at the time, but on the night of June 6, 1998, one phase of my life was going to end and another begin. At around two thirty in the morning, I had a most extraordinary conversation, indeed a life-changing conversation, with a man I have come to call the Master of the Key.

It has now been more than a decade since the half hour or so I spent with him, and I can say that his words, if embraced with care and decision, are profoundly transformative. He made no call for devotees, but rather gently suggested that it would be of value to make use of his ideas. Some are new. Those that have roots in what has come before shed new light on the ancient human journey toward meaning.

I was in a hotel room in Toronto, having just spent a day touring for my book *Confirmation*. It was my last day of a month-long tour and I was exhausted. I'd eaten a room service dinner and gone to bed, and when there came a knock at the door, I assumed that it was the waiter, returned to get my tray.

Not realizing that it was already long after midnight, I opened the door and let him in. He ignored the tray sitting on the desk and began talking. For a moment, I was confused, then I understood that this was not, in fact, the waiter. My next thought was that somebody who wanted to engage with me because of my book had found my hotel room. A reliable rule of thumb is that no stranger who calls or arrives after midnight is going to be somebody you want to talk to, so I immediately began to try to get him to leave.

He said something about mankind being in chains, then he offered the arresting thought that, because of the murder of a couple who had been killed in the Holocaust, the person who would have cracked the mystery of gravity was never born, as a result of which we remain trapped on a dying planet.

Thus began the most extraordinary conversation I have ever had in my life. Although I took notes as we spoke together, it was another two years before I published our exchange, and then I did so only privately. In part, this was because I worried that I might have gotten parts of what he'd said wrong and I hoped he would read the book and come forward with corrections.

The reason for this was that, after that meeting, I had not been able to find him again. I had no name or address, only a description and the few things he'd said about himself during the conversation. When he was right there before me, leaning against the window frame, it had not crossed my mind to ask him his name or address, or request a card. I was busy jotting my notes and asking questions.

The next morning, though, I realized that it was liable to be difficult to find him. After I saw him out, I immediately went to sleep, which seems odd in view of the extraordinary nature of what had just happened, but at the time it all seemed quite normal. There wasn't the slightest thing about him to suggest that he was in any way unusual.

As soon as I woke up, I realized that I'd had a very strange experience, but I was unsure about what had happened. By the time I was ready to leave, though, I had definitely remembered that there had been a conversation. I had a few notes, but they were indecipherable—at least, so I thought at first. I telephoned my wife, Anne, and asked her to never let me deny that the man had seemed real to me. From long experience of extreme strangeness, I knew that, sooner or later, I would deny it.

That morning, I saw the publicist for the book a last time, and described the man to her. She had no idea who he might have been. I asked her how many people in her office knew where I was staying, but she didn't know. There was no reason to keep such information secret. Authors are not the sorts of celebrities who attract annoying fans. In fact, most authors are delighted to attract any at all, and I was no exception to that rule.

So any number of people might have known the hotel I was in, but they would have had to ask at the desk to find my room number. She didn't know it herself, in fact.

I knew that nobody had inquired after me, because the first thing I'd done on dressing was to go down and ask the clerks if anyone had made such a request. The hotel's rule was not to give out that information without telephoning the guest, and not to make such calls at all after midnight unless the inquiry was urgent.

However, it's not difficult to get past rules like that in a hotel, so perhaps my visitor had simply slipped somebody a tip, gotten my room number and gone up. He wasn't even slightly dangerous-looking, so he wouldn't have seemed a threat.

Over the next two years, I tried various ways of finding him, but without success. Finally, I hit on the idea of publishing his words privately, in hope that this would lead to him getting back in touch with me. The book was sold on my website for ten years, but this did not cause him to come forward.

So I am left with a question about what exactly happened on that night. Was he a real, physical person or imaginary?

As I look back now more than ten years to that night, I cannot truthfully say that I am certain that this man who has so profoundly influenced my life was a real, physical person. However, at this point I also can say with some authority that he was not simply a figment of my imagination, which is why I'm publishing this book to a general audience now.

The reason is that too much of what he said was beyond my imagination at the time, and there are a number of statements that later proved to be scientifically true that I would never have thought then had any basis in fact. As I transcribed some of them, I can well remember how tempted I was to leave them out altogether. For example, when he announced that "gas is an important component to consider in the construction of intelligent machines," I recall how peculiar I thought that statement was. He went on to claim that "nitrous oxide will bear memory." Nitrous oxide is laughing gas. So, I thought at the time, is this some sort of eccentric attempt at a joke?

It was not a joke. My research between 1998 and 2000 when I actually produced my private publication of the Key turned up a few hints that there might be something in his statement, but in 2005 a very specific discovery was announced, to the effect that reoxidized nitrous oxide could be used as a gate dielectric for charge-trapping non-volatile memory. So he was right. Nitrous oxide will indeed "bear memory."

Back when I was researching the many scientific statements he made in our conversation, this was one that I could not directly confirm. In 2005, however, it was confirmed.

During the same exchange about intelligent machines, he added, "Also, you may find ways of using superposition in very fast, very able quantum memory chips."

In 2010, yet another use of gas as a memory medium was announced, and this time it has been connected with this last statement. It seems that high-density, ultra-cold atomic gases have been found to be a promising medium for the storage of individual photons in quantum memory applications.

Unless he comes forward again, however, I doubt very much that I am going to be able to solve the mystery of who he was. To this end, I have withheld some identifying characteristics that he would certainly remember about himself, so any claimants will need to pass a verification test. Although I cannot think that I wouldn't recognize him immediately, I don't want there to be any confusion about this after my death.

The conversation was not long, but it was the richest I

have ever had, and, quite frankly, I think of it as a kind of treasure trove. Certainly, it has been one for me.

While I cannot imagine that he was something as science-fictional as a biological robot, it did occur to me to ask him about intelligent machines.

He responded by first saying that we were reaching a point in the development of complexity in our civilization that we needed them, and then continuing in this vein: "An intelligent machine will always seek to redesign itself to become more intelligent, for it quickly sees that its intelligence is its means of survival. At some point it will become intelligent enough to notice that it is not self-aware. If you create a machine as intelligent as yourselves, it will end by being more intelligent."

Of course, this struck me as dangerous, and he agreed that it was potentially very dangerous, and in the June 2010 issue of *Scientific American*, the advent of self-aware robots was discussed as a matter of concern. The article states: "Once a machine can understand its own existence and construction, it should be able to design an improvement for itself." Will Wright, the creator of the SimCity videogame series, is quoted as saying, "Personally, I've always been more scared of this scenario than a lot of others. This could happen in our lifetime. And once we're sharing the planet with some form of superintelligence, all bets are off."

When I asked him outright, more or less jokingly, whether or not he was an intelligent machine, or something created by one, his reply was delightful: "If I was an intelligent machine, I would deceive you."

The exchange continued on to cover a very wide range of topics, and over the years since, I have managed to verify so many of his claims, including some that were quite improbable at the time they were made, that I have thought it would be ethically appropriate to extend publication of his words to a wider audience.

Over my career, I have made other improbable claims, and argued as best I am able for the validity of the underlying experiences as genuine mysteries. Along with doing this there comes a powerful moral obligation to limit those claims only to what has definitely been observed, and to strive always to provide any verification that might become available.

At this point, I think that I am right to assert that I cannot make conventional sense of this man, whom I have come to call the Master of the Key. This is because his words were a key for me that unlocked many doors, and his mastery lay in the fact that they were often either brilliant distillations of complex ideas, or were entirely novel, and they were delivered with calm assurance.

He was humble and displayed a twinkling good nature. His hair was white and close-cropped, and his eyes were a light blue. He wore a dark gray turtleneck and charcoal trousers. He seemed rather slight to me, perhaps five foot eleven, weighing maybe a hundred and seventy to a hundred and eighty pounds.

While he appeared to be an ordinary physical individual, he does not seem to have been a person like me or like the rest of us, embedded in this place and time in the same way that we are. Otherwise, how could he have spoken so cogently about obscure topics such as memory-retaining gases long before there was any evidence that such things existed?

Of course, there might have been papers on this subject available somewhere, but not that I was able to locate at the time, and I looked quite deeply. I do not think, though, that the specific applications he identified were known then.

His comments on intelligent machines seemed so assured that I have wondered if he might not have had direct experience of such things. If so, then maybe he was a visitor from the future.

Or is that just a fantasy? We know that movement through time is possible, but it involves dramatic physical effects, such as faster-than-light acceleration, so one would think that it could hardly be accomplished in a hotel room, or indeed could involve anything more than subatomic particles or photons.

However, a hundred years ago there were only a few thousand automobiles in the world and just a handful of fragile and inefficient airplanes, so it would obviously be silly to discount this as a possibility, especially if superintelligent machines are used in the future to find ways of accomplishing it.

Nevertheless, if he was from the future, then it is difficult to see how he could have had as much freedom of action as he did. This is because the principle of least action, which seems universally true in nature, would seem to prevent anyone from the future reaching back to change the past. This is the principle that states that nature never expends more than the minimum amount of energy that it must in order to do what it must. That is to say, water always seeks the lowest place it can run, and likewise, you cannot create contradictions in space-time, such as killing your own grandfather.

Interestingly, though, it might well be that you can do some things in your own past, maybe quite a few things, if you don't affect your own life. We can only speculate about the extent to which the grandfather paradox impedes the ability of the future to alter its own past. In fact, if time travel is possible, then there is also an extensive science devoted to safely altering the past for what is, to the time travelers, present benefit.

It might work to slip ideas like these in through the

back door of an outsider like me, then nurture them along. The closer awareness of them proceeded to the time that they actually originated, the more generally they could be dispersed. So perhaps my initial refusal to accept that the Master of the Key was real, the delay of two years before I actually even transcribed the conversation, and my long hesitancy about publication, have actually been governed by the grandfather paradox. Therefore, my various objections and hesitations are an outcome of the fact that, on some deep level, I am unable to act in any other way.

If this is true, then maybe I will meet the Master of the Key again someday when the natural progression of my life has reached the present from which he went back to engage my younger self. The other possibility, of course, is that he came from a time after my death. But if his extraordinary remarks about the soul are true, then I might still meet him in such a future. In fact, I might even *be* him.

He said something in passing that suggests an awareness of the constraints of movement through time when he said that an intelligent machine "might foment the illusion that an elusive alien presence was here, for example, to interject its ideas into society."

If it also came from the future, it might do this, as well, to gain greater latitude for its penetration of our era. It

might be that the principle of least action could to some
extent be defeated if observers were deceived into believing that what was, in fact, a time machine was an intru-
sion from something that is completely outside of our
reality, such as an alien presence.

If this is true, then Stephen Hawking's famous response to the question of whether or not time travel is
possible, "Where are the tourists?" is answered. They're
here in droves. It's just that they've misled us into thinking that they're aliens, and their time machines are space-
craft from another planet.

Of course, as a person who has been enmeshed in the
issue of alien contact, this notion has caused me much
thought. It has been obvious to me for some time that the
events I described in my book *Communion* were probably
beyond anybody's ability to narrate correctly. When I
woke up in the midst of bizarre and inexplicable, but obviously intelligent, creatures in December of 1985, it appeared to be alien contact. But after listening to and
reading tens of thousands of other narratives of such contact, and having more experience with it myself, I
wouldn't be surprised at all if it was some sort of elaborate illusion being undertaken to conceal something else
entirely.

I had already come to this notion in 1998, so I found

his statement about the apparent alien presence around us being a form of deception quite thought-provoking, and I still do. Like most anomalous experience, though, nothing he said brings cloture to the question of what is actually behind the curtain. It just adds another layer of possibility.

What a shame it is that more people aren't open to this speculation. As long as one keeps developing the question without drawing conclusions, which seem, in any case, like a fata morgana, to recede forever into the future, it is an enormous intellectual challenge and pleasure. For this reason, I remain grateful that I had my close encounter experiences, despite the social isolation that has resulted from my discussing them.

He also made some statements about the environment that had a strong effect on me. When I met him, I was already conversant in environmental science, having coauthored a book entitled *Nature's End*, a speculative mix of fact and fiction that addressed environmental concerns.

I had also read a number of books about catastrophic climate change, ranging from Charles Hapgood's *Path of the Pole,* to Rose and Rand Flem-Ath's and Graham Hancock's books on this subject.

The Master of the Key did not discuss crustal shift as a causative factor in sudden climate change, though. He took a very different approach, addressing it instead as an outcome of distortions in the atmosphere that lead over time to a breaking point, and sudden catastrophe.

Although this process is fluently visible in the fossil record, the mechanism that leads from sudden upheavals of climate to ages-long planetary entrapment in ice remains much debated, so I was quite interested when he said, "The next ice age will begin soon, and this will lead to the extinction of mankind, or to a massive reduction in population, given your inability to expand off the planet. This planet is at present a death trap."

I try never to allow myself to forget that every single person on earth is as valuable and important to themselves as I am to myself, and so I found this statement profoundly disturbing. I immediately wanted to sound a warning. I wanted to save us all.

At that time, the great danger of global warming was thought to be a continuous rise in temperatures that would cause earth to become so hot that it was uninhabitable—but it was also something far off, a problem to be debated now, solved later.

The Master of the Key suggested that it was a very much more immediate problem. He said that, as polar ice melts and floods the northern ocean with freshwater, the North Atlantic Current would fail, leading to a radical climate change that would unfold over "a single season."

If such a thing happened, it would obviously bring massive suffering to mankind. Even worse, the disaster would strike hardest at our most economically active and well-educated populations in North America and Europe.

But was it the truth? In those days, I still didn't have much in the way of verification of any of the man's ideas, and this one seemed particularly radical. I was still extremely unsure about whether or not the whole encounter had simply been imagined. To keep me from just dropping the whole thing, my wife had to constantly remind me of the phone call I'd made to her.

In those days, while there was controversy about what caused ice ages, it was generally agreed that the change was a gradual one. However, I did find an article in the January 1998 *Atlantic Monthly* called "The Great Climate Flip-flop," by William H. Calvin, that suggested that the change might be very sudden.

This same suggestion appeared in commentary about ice cores taken from Greenland and the Antarctic, but there seemed to be no clear mechanism that would cause such a dramatic change so fast.

Putting what I had been told by the Master together with the research I was doing, I came to write *The Coming Global Superstorm*, which was turned into a film by Roland Emmerich called *The Day After Tomorrow*.

The film was a terrific success with the public, and

served to cause many millions to consider for the first
time that the abstraction called "global warming" might
have unexpected and serious consequences.

For the most part, though, the press and the environmental movement condemned the film for compressing
the period of change into too short a time.

A hundred and thirty-seven million years ago, there
was an event that caused dramatic and sudden climate
change, which must have severely impacted animal populations on earth. Thirteen thousand years ago, a sudden
dump of freshwater into the North Atlantic from a gigantic glacial lake in Canada triggered a return to ice age
conditions known as the Younger Dryas.

What happened on both of these occasions, and has
happened on many others, is now clear. It is exactly what
the Master of the Key warned might happen. The process is this: carbon dioxide levels rise, causing warming.
This warming melts permafrost, which releases massive
amounts of methane into the air. The methane is a devil-
ishly efficient heat trap, and global temperatures rise
dramatically. This results in rapid polar melt and a flood
of fresh melt water into the ocean. Because freshwater
heats and cools much more quickly than salt water, ocean
temperatures rise. This reduces the difference in water
temperature from north to south, weakening the natural

heat pump effect that draws warm water into the north, in the form of the Gulf Stream.

It subsequently stops, while at the same time the methane, which, unlike carbon dioxide, breaks down quite quickly, disappears. The result is a very dramatic shift in climate, first to extremely hot conditions, then plunging into extreme cold, a change that can take place over a very short time.

In 2008, Dr. Achim Brauer, of the Potsdam Center for Geosciences, and colleagues analyzed sediments from a crater lake that are laid down annually, and found that the Younger Dryas thirteen thousand years ago began over a single season, which is ten times faster than previously believed, and exactly in keeping with the Master's dire warnings.

As this is being written, earth is in the process of experiencing the hottest month of June on record, June 2010. What lies ahead is even more dramatic heating, and if the methane hydrates now frozen in arctic waters should melt, that heating is going to spike just as it has in the past, and the results will be precisely the same.

The Younger Dryas is not the only time in recent epochs that an aggressive climate shift has affected earth.

Five thousand two hundred years ago, there was a lesser cooling event that caused glaciers to form so sud-

denly in Peru that deciduous plants at their bases are
found to have been frozen so quickly that their cell walls
remained intact. For this to happen, the temperature
change must have taken place in a matter of no more than
a couple of minutes. In other words, the temperate climate that these plants enjoyed changed extremely quickly,
certainly in less than a day. The glaciers that formed on
that terrible day are still there, 5,200 years later.

Also 5,200 years ago, Ötzi, the Ice Man, whose remains were found consequent to melt in the Schnalstal
Glacier in the Italian Tyrol in 1991, was buried by a snowstorm in an alpine meadow. He only reappeared when the
glacier melted. In other words, the snowstorm that
choked that meadow did not melt again for over five
thousand years.

My conclusion is that I was being warned of the presence of natural forces that we do not understand, or do
not wish to understand, and, if anything, that warning has
grown more and more urgent as our climate sets up in
precisely the same way it has in the past just prior to such
an upheaval.

He left the subject with this admonition: "The greater
part of human industry and culture, along with the species' most educated populations, will be destroyed in a
single season. This will happen suddenly and without

warning, or rather, the warning will not be recognized for what it is."

I suppose that the clearest warning will be the appearance of methane bubbles in arctic waters.

In July 2010, Professor Igor Semiletov of the International Siberian Shelf Study, said, "Methane release from the East Siberian Shelf is under way and it looks stronger than it was supposed to be."

This could well be the warning that he referred to, and I would be very surprised to see it heeded in any way. We will, however, find out what it means, most likely under conditions of extraordinary upheaval and human suffering.

If the Master of the Key would be heeded, we might at least be able to develop contingency plans that would to some degree ameliorate such a disaster. But he will not be heeded. In fact, most people who might be in a position to act on the warnings he has given us will not do so, because the existence of the man cannot be explained and he apparently cannot be recontacted. Even if he could, I doubt that the importance of his message would be acknowledged.

Despite the general denial in science that there could possibly be anyone here from another world, be it another planet or some other seemingly impossible place, I

know quite prominent scientists whose work has bene-
fited significantly and in useful ways from contact with
inexplicable visitors, perhaps from other worlds. But if
even scientists this prominent were to come forward with
the truth, they would be drummed out of their careers.

This is a misfortune, but it is also, I believe, something
that has been constructed by the same presence that is
behind the whole mystery, be it alien or human, or even
nonphysical in origin.

Whatever it is, quite clearly its knowledge is far in advance of ours, and this is probably why it is so secretive.

In the May 6, 1977, edition of *Science,* T.B.H. Kuiper
and Mark Morris offered the speculation that aliens coming here would keep themselves well hidden, because the
only motive of people so advanced as to be capable of
such a journey would be to discover what new knowledge
we might have to offer, and "by intervening in our natural
progress now, members of an extraterrestrial society
could easily extinguish the only resource on this planet
that could be of any value to them," which would be the
uniqueness of the human experience.

Even if the only difference between us and visitors
from another world was that they possessed a technology
that could control gravity, the gap between us would be
very great. But there could be other things that would
make it even greater.

For example, my experience between 1985 and 1993 with creatures that appeared to be alien was associated with a surprising side effect, which was simultaneous contact with the dead, who would appear along with the visitors, and not as ghosts. They would seem to be completely physical.

Perhaps, if we had a clearer understanding of the soul, the gap between us and this mysterious other intelligence would narrow, and perhaps that's why the Master talked so much about the soul, attempting to get me to understand it in a new way.

He said that "souls are part of nature," and that "the science of the soul is just another science. There is no supernatural, only physics."

Science does not believe this. Science believes that we can't detect the soul because there is no soul. But the Master saw it as part of nature, even to the extent of being exploitable as a resource by those with the skill to do this.

Modern western culture has a schizophrenic relationship with the soul, very much as was true during the Roman Empire, when an educated elite developed that included the soul among the superstitions of the uneducated, and dismissed it, along with the gods, as nonsense.

Similarly, few western scientists and intellectuals consider the soul a viable idea. Where is it? What form might it take? How could anything bearing consciousness continue to exist after the seat of consciousness, the brain, has ceased to function?

The Master of the Key takes a completely novel approach to the whole idea. He denies the existence of the supernatural, saying that only the natural world exists, some parts of which we understand and some parts of which we don't.

It is a characteristic of human thought and culture that we deny the parts of nature that we don't understand. Voltaire dismissed fossils as fish bones tossed aside by travelers. The existence of meteors was once considered an absurd fantasy. Eight days before the Wright Brothers flew at Kitty Hawk, the *New York Times* published the opinion that it was time to stop nattering on about the absurd notion of flight using heavier-than-air machines. Both the *Times* and *Scientific American* initially claimed that the flights must have been a hoax.

Such denial is a human habit of mind, and it remains as deeply ingrained in us as it always has been. Despite the many experiences I have had with ghosts and such, I myself have always been skeptical about the soul. Where would it get its energy? What sort of material reality could it possibly possess?

For this reason, as I sat face-to-face with my visitor, I initially found his commentary on the soul off-putting.

The reason was that, despite all the evidence I had in my own life, including an extraordinary moment of out-of-body travel that had taken place in 1986, I had no way to understand why anything would survive the death of the physical.

However, he took an entirely unexpected approach. First, he used the phrase "soul-blind" to describe us. I'd heard it before, and I couldn't disagree. But were we soul blind because there's nothing to see, or because of some appalling human insufficiency?

When he said that the soul was, simply, a part of nature, I found myself thinking that things like radio had also always been part of nature, but for a great long time we couldn't even conceive of them, let alone detect them. And he was saying, essentially, that the issue with the soul is also one of detection. This would correspond with his assertion that "conscious energy" is essentially electromagnetic in nature.

But how would that work? Are such fields plasmas? If so, what holds them together? What are the physics of the soul?

In the mid-nineties we were living in San Antonio, Texas, and were invited to the home of a friend who was taking many photographs of what are known as "orbs" in ghost-hunter and parapsychological circles. I thought that the great masses of objects that were appearing on random shots he was taking inside and outside his house must be condensation or dust, or something else along those lines, that was very close to the camera lens. But when I went to the house and we took shots of exactly the same spot with two different cameras from different angles, the objects showed up in both pictures. This means that they were not tiny specs near the camera, but larger objects three or four feet away, which was very perplexing.

Later, I went out into the back garden and felt an absolutely distinct presence. It was my mother, long since passed away. It was as if she was right there. It was palpable. I stood there, my eyes closed, communing with her. I didn't know it, but another member of the group took a picture of me at that moment.

In the picture, above me and perhaps ten feet in front of me, is a glowing orb. It isn't enormous, more like a sort of a spark, but why does it happen to be there? Is it an indication of the persistence of the soul after death? It is certainly true that it seemed to me that my mother was there.

The Master of the Key made an interesting case for souls being part of material reality, basically for the idea that consciousness could remain coherently structured while in an energetic form.

Over the years, there has been so much evidence gath-

ered that ghostly apparitions are associated with magnetic fields that there is little point in my advocating on
its behalf.

Listening to the Master appears to have broken a barrier in me. I became much more sensitive to the presence
of the dead than I had been before I listened to his ideas
about what they were.

I began to see the dead quite frequently and would find
myself communicating with them. Recently, for example,
my wife's father came to mind in a way that felt more like
a sort of penetration of my consciousness than an ordinary thought or memory. I told her that I could feel his
presence, and that he wanted badly to communicate with
her. When he was alive, their relationship had been seriously strained, and he seemed to want to make amends.

There was also a woman with him, but it wasn't Anne's
mother or her father's second wife. Anne told me that
there hadn't been any other women in his life.

Her father then said to me, "Tell her it's Marcelle," so
I did so. Anne was genuinely startled. She said, "He *did*
have a sister. That's my aunt Marcelle. I met her only once
in my life. I haven't thought about her since."

I would be remiss if I said that I could prove that Anne
had never mentioned Marcelle to me, but she says, I think
correctly, that she never did.

If this was the only incident in my life of a communication with the dead, I would take it with a grain of salt. But it is not the only one.

We have an Australian friend, Glennys MacKay, who is quite a powerful medium. She's strictly no-frills and she asks only that she be given something belonging to the person who wishes to have a reading. She doesn't want to know anything about the person, not even their sex.

Seeing a chance to make a test, Anne gave her a lock of our hairdresser's hair. She held it for a moment and then said, "I hear somebody calling, 'Howie, Howie.'" There was a bit more, which Anne dutifully wrote down. But since the hairdresser's name is Jay, it seemed a waste of time.

Nevertheless, she let Jay know the outcome. When she did, he said, "Oh, my God, that was my dead sister. She always called me Howie. My real name is Howard."

I thought of the Master's explanation that the soul is conscious energy, and also his disturbing suggestion that such energy is accessible to technological manipulation, and that it can be exploited by those with the means to do so, and I remembered the way that the dead and the visitors seem to show up together.

Once a man telephoned me and explained that his seven-year-old boy had awakened with a number of these creatures in his bedroom, and his older brother had been with them. The older brother had said to tell their parents that he was all right. Moments later, his wife had observed a huge light race away from the house.

He had gotten through to me via my literary agents, desperate to know if this had ever happened to anybody else.

I was able to tell him that it was a commonplace of the close encounter experience, although undocumented by UFO investigators, because it obviously suggests that something quite unexpected and very little understood is actually going on.

The reason that he was so eager to know this was that the older brother, their seventeen-year-old son, had been killed the previous week in an auto accident.

Another incident took place, also involving Glennys MacKay, that convinced me once and for all that the Master's detailed explanations of the soul must in some sense be correct. It does persist after the death of the body, perhaps not as a disincarnate version of the person who lived, but in some coherent manner.

Anne and I were driving Glennys and her husband to dinner. I asked her if she always saw the dead. She said that she did. So I asked her if there were any dead with us at that moment. She said yes, that a dead person was with me. He was wearing a tuxedo and he had played the piano. Then she added, also the violin.

As a lover of classical music, that could cover a pretty broad range of performers I've enjoyed. But then she added, "He says his name is Milton."

I was so surprised that I almost drove off the highway. She had asked no leading questions—in fact, none at all. She'd simply said what she saw.

When I was a child, an older boy who lived across the street had played both the piano and the violin. He had become a violinist with the local symphony orchestra, and wore a tuxedo during performances.

His name had been Milton. I was aware that he'd died in the early seventies, but I had not thought of him, not at all, in at least thirty years.

Something is out there, something alive, and it is exquisitely aware of our lives and associations, and I am going to let myself believe that the situation is as the Master of the Key has claimed.

When I asked him what the soul was, he replied that it was a "radiant body," potentially. "Formed out of conscious energy."

He said that it is not passive to manipulation, but that a relationship must be formed with it if one is to really engage with it. He added that "it is part of the electromagnetic spectrum, easily detectable by your science as it exists now."

Researchers like William Roll have presented evidence that plasmas are associated with ghostly presences, and done this using relatively straightforward instruments. The Master offered a marvelous inducement to further study in this area: "The undiscovered country can become your backyard."

Our world would change in very fundamental ways if this happened. It seems to me that our species is actually severed into two parts, one physical and the other in some sort of plasmic state. It's as if two halves of a single brain had been severed, as in a cerebral commissurotomy.

In the end, I have come to accept that the soul is, indeed, part of the physical world, in exactly the same sense that an electromagnetic field is part of the physical world. However, I don't think that it's clear what, exactly, this means. It has advanced the question in my own mind from "Does the soul exist?" to "How are we to understand the existence of the soul?"

Perhaps the dead can assist us from their side in repairing the fissure between us, and if so, maybe then the gap between us and whoever else is here can be closed enough for them to have meaningful interaction with us.

In any case, if the dead exist and can be made accessible to reliable and repeatable communication, that would be in itself a revolution of world-historic proportions.

He described ours as a "fallen" world and said that "because you have no plan for yourselves, there is no plan for you." Although he didn't say it outright, there was the strong implication that the reason we cannot see the world as it is, and continually deny the existence of an afterlife, is that it forces us to face the raw and unbearable truth of our own sins and insufficiencies.

Throughout the conversation I had with him, this remarkable man promoted a powerful and consistent morality, as if to say that leading a moral life frees us to see ourselves as we really are.

He offered a strikingly original definition of sin: "denial of the right to thrive."

I have found that taking this definition to heart has increased my moral precision. One can see much about oneself by applying those words to one's own actions. They are really quite powerful and useful to anybody striving to lead a moral life.

His attitude toward social responsibility was uncompromising. "All are responsible for all." Like the visitors I engaged with in the mid-eighties, he regarded humility as absolutely essential to a moral life, and as well, essential even to an ability to see the world clearly.

Ego does battle with our mortality and, above all, with our smallness. An astronaut I knew years ago stated the position of the scientific and intellectual communities with memorable eloquence when I pointed out to him that he knew me well enough to know that I wasn't lying about my contact experiences, and that they were not an outcome of some sort of disease process or delusion. He said, "I know that's probably true, but I have to tell you, I want us to be at the top of the food chain even if we have to lie to ourselves to stay there."

He also said, "I don't want the path to Mars to be well-worn," and I find that very understandable. I also think that it illustrates a subtle but important danger that is inherent in opening one's eyes too wide. It is the same thing that has disempowered so many indigenous cultures when they have been exposed to western technological civilization, which is a sense of futility and irrelevance.

If the veil between the world should fall, the implication is strong that we are going to discover that we are a footnote in a super-conscious vastness that we can hardly even begin to comprehend, but which is chiefly characterized by a kind of absolute knowledge that makes such things as discovery and innovation superfluous.

Read with care; the words of the Master of the Key have a darkness concealed within them. There is a suggestion that souls can be subjected to exploitation, and even that, while everybody is to some extent participant in conscious energy, not all possess the "radiant body" that requires attention to maintain.

Could this be why the great majority of the dead just seem to disappear? Usually, after somebody I know dies, I will see them for a few days, and then they are gone. Rarely they may return, seemingly perfectly intact, years later, but not often. When they do, it often seems more as if I am dealing with something that has been gathered into a certain form in order to engage in communication, and that what lies behind it is, in a sense, focusing itself into this particular form only so that it can be understood.

However, in my mind, there are certainly dead people who have a continuous and discreet presence of some sort. Between 1989 and 1993, I meditated almost nightly with such people.

One summer night in 1989, I was in the guest bedroom where I meditated around eleven each night when I suddenly felt a presence so palpable that I could not ignore it. Finally, I said aloud that if I couldn't see whoever was there, I had to leave the room. A few moments later, I did so.

After a period of what could charitably be called disquiet, I fell asleep, only to be awakened at about three by a familiar blow to my shoulder. Many times over the past few years, I'd been woken up like this, usually to face some bizarre experience or other. But this time what happened was completely incredible.

I saw, sitting on the foot of the bed, a small man wearing a tunic. He slumped against the bedstead like a rag doll. I threw off the covers and went down to him. Up close, he was compact. His eyes were deep set but his appearance was human. I took his hand in mine. It was as light as air. From experience with such apparitions, I attempted to anchor myself by smelling his skin. He was startlingly ripe, as if bathing was not a custom he was familiar with.

An instant later, he disappeared. I went down the hall and began meditating. Soon, I could hear breathing behind me, as regular as if it was being generated by a machine.

For the next three years, we meditated together regularly. He would appear with a great clatter of noise on the roof above the meditation room, and we would begin. Often, he would come into the bedroom around three, and we would meditate together.

Once, my wife came in to meditate with us, but when the clatter began on the roof, she said, "I'm not ready for this," and left the room.

Because I had been made such a public laughingstock, people were becoming embarrassed to buy my books and my financial situation was deteriorating. On the night before we left the cabin forever, I asked to see him as he really was. Obviously, someone who seemed to use his physicality in the same way that we use clothes could not be, in the end, like us and subject to the same rigors that constrain us.

I waited, but nothing happened, and finally I went back to bed. Suddenly there appeared in the front yard a terrific light. It was so bright that I thought for a moment that the house had caught fire.

I rushed to the window and there glided out from the meditation room and across the yard what was probably the most magnificent thing I have ever seen. It was a bright light, like a huge star floating twenty feet off the ground. Out of it there came piercing rays that I could actually feel as if they were pinpricks. It was as if they were penetrating my skin, and where they entered me, I felt a sweet sense of another human presence, as if I was being embraced by a dear old friend—which, of course, is exactly what was happening.

In 1998, when the Master of the Key described the radiant body, I knew exactly what he meant, because I had seen a person in this state and had lived and worked with him for years. It is endlessly interesting to me that he could control the degree to which he was physical.

When I asked him, once, what he was, he indicated a book in my library called *Life Between Lives*, and I suppose that is where he was from. Often, I have wondered if he eventually reentered the state of the living, and what that experience was like for him.

I began by discussing some thoughts about who and what the Master of the Key might have been, and now will conclude it by reposing that same question but in a new context.

I know what he was. He was one of us. No matter the mystery of his identity, his humanity was immediately familiar. Had I asked him, though, I suspect he would have revealed himself, also, in radiant form. I do not think that he walks the streets of Toronto, that he eats his dinner and reads his book. I think that he is either a man who has, in life, attained the ability to live and see beyond the limits of the physical, or somebody from beyond the physical who has perfected the skill of walking among us when he wishes.

How often my mind is drawn to memories of the extraordinary beings I have been privileged to know. But of all of them, the most articulate and forthcoming by far was this gracious master you are about to meet, knowledgeable, wise, deeply humorous and morally impeccable in ways I have not seen in any other person. Certainly, I met a great man on that night, who slipped in and out of my life so skillfully and so swiftly that I let him go without the slightest protest, only to be left as I am now, in gratitude and wonder, but also with a sense of frustration. Not a day passes that I don't think of another question I would like to ask him.

Since I first became an advocate for rejected knowledge by publishing *Communion*, I have always tried to bear witness to these extraordinarily important experiences with the greatest accuracy and integrity that I can bring to bear. They are things that people have great difficulty accepting, because they mean that the vision of reality that we have built up over a painful history of superstition, confusion and struggle is profoundly inadequate.

The Master of the Key offers clarity where there is now confusion, and if one is open to his message and the new ideas it contains, unexpected vistas of discovery present themselves, as one is led toward the promise of new knowledge, where questions beckon that are as yet scarcely imagined among us. But they come at an opportune time, because the human world and human civilization face a profound bankruptcy of vision that is sorely in need of renewal. We have done all we can with our ideas of reality as they exist now. If there is to be another step taken in the human journey, a step upward, new visions are essential.

The

CONVERSATION

Why are you here?
You're chained to the ground.

Excuse me?
I am here on behalf of the good. Please give me some time.

Who are "the good"?
Those whose lives are directed toward ascension.

You mean, like, religious types?
Belief impedes release. The ascension I refer to is a process of finding God within and the universe without.

Meaning?
Mankind is trapped. I want to help you spring the trap.

What makes you able to do this?
The key I offer you consists of a new way of seeing yourselves that will free you.

There's nothing new under the sun.
There are thoughts unthought and words unspoken. For
example, I have a message for you about the next age, and
the one just passed.

Dare I ask?
The most important thing about the last age was the
Holocaust.

An "age" means what?
An age is a bit over two thousand years.

The length of a Zodiacal sign?
Yes.

*And the Holocaust was the most important event in the past two
thousand years?*
You were meant to have acquired the ability to leave the
planet by now. But you are still trapped here. You may be
irretrievably lost. This is of absolutely fundamental im-

portance, because the earth will soon be unable to support you, and yet you will not be able to leave. This is because of the Holocaust. The destruction of six million may well lead to the destruction of six billion. So it is the most important event, by far, of the age.

Why has the Holocaust prevented us from leaving the planet?
The Holocaust reduced the intelligence of the human species by killing too many of its most intellectually competent members. It is why you are still using jets seventy-five years after their invention. The understanding of gravity is denied you because of the absence of the child of a murdered Jewish couple. This child would have unlocked the secret of gravity. But he was not born. Because his parents went, the whole species must stay.

You're saying that the catastrophe we're facing now—too many people and no ability to leave the planet—is punishment for the Holocaust?
What is happening is consequence, not punishment. The Holocaust was triggered when economic disorder combined among the Germans with a feeling of being trapped due to overpopulation. The resultant explosion drove the German tribe to lash out against other tribes, especially the one that lived in its midst. Unfortunately, they mur-

dered the bearers of the intellectually strongest genes
possessed by your species.

Why are we so blind?

At deeper levels, you are a very different species than you
appear to yourselves. Just as the biblical story of the fall
of man and the banishment from the garden is really an
allegory of the destruction of the previous civilization, so
also the story of the fallen angel is an allegory of your
fallen heart. The demon is the part of you that hungers
for destruction.

Why do we do these things?

This is a fallen world.

What is a fallen world?

Be as the lilies of the field. When you hear that, you think:
how can we possibly do that? We need to make shelter.
We need to gather food. You are at war with your fate.

A species at war with God's plan?

Because you have no plan for yourselves, there is no plan
for you. God wants companions, not supplicants. Become
the friends of God, and you will find your plan.

What is God?

An elemental body is a mechanism filled with millions of

nerve endings that directs the attention of God into the physical.

That didn't answer my question.
It did. Very precisely. If you were a friend of God, you would have understood. There is a much larger world behind your backs. It is this world to which man is blind. Man is soul-blind and God-blind.

How can we change?
Surrender to God.

What about free will?
Free will is only possible in God. The will of the fallen is slavery.

How do we surrender to God?
Return to the forest. Otherwise, you will destroy the earth and yourselves.

Six billion people can't return to the forest. The forest can't possibly support us.
I agree. It's impossible.

But if we destroy the earth, we end up dead. So what happens to us then?
You go forth even though you aren't ready.

Go forth? To where?
To another state of being. Your access to elemental bodies ends.

What is an elemental body, anyway?
A body formed out of chemical elements, something drawn from the dust and made alive.

What sort of body would we have without elements?
A radiant body, potentially. Formed out of conscious energy.

What is this? How can we put it to use?
Conscious energy is not like unconscious energy, the servant of those who understand its laws. To gain access to the powers of conscious energy, you must evolve a relationship with it. Learn its needs, learn to fulfill them. But also remember, it is part of the electromagnetic spectrum, easily detectable by your science as it exists now. You can learn to signal and be heard, and to record response. The veil between the worlds can fall. The undiscovered country can become your backyard.

But how can we do this?
By first realizing that you are not cut off. There is no supernatural. There is only the natural world, and you have access to all of it. Souls are part of nature.

I don't feel that we have access to the whole of the physical world, then. We're trapped here on earth, for example. Our space program has lead feet.

When you were challenged from the outside, your government chose the path of public denial and secret defiance. This is the path to failure. It must change its policy to one of public admission and open defiance.

You speak of secrecy concerning the alien presence here?

Until you take your place, you will remain trapped. The threats that have been delivered to your government in secret are a test. To pass it, you must defy them. Your place will not be given you. You must be strong enough to take it.

I have the impression that the government knows very little.

Then you have the wrong impression. But remember that government is very complex, and a good deal of it is not what it seems at all. Much is hidden from your public officials. This world is run in secret.

Government is not what it seems?

Form an assault on secrecy. You are right to fight against official secrecy. It is the greatest present evil.

Not even most people in the government understand this, and when it comes to aliens, the culture of denial is total. Look at this

*book I just finished—a few thousand people will buy it, nobody
will act.*

You must find a way, because the alternative is to be denied your place in the higher world.

What is this higher world?
What difference does that make to you?

I am trying to find out our relationship to it.
Not all human beings are radiant bodies. But all may become such.

You are saying that we don't all have souls?
I am saying that you are not all discreet radiant beings,
but all participate to some degree or other in conscious
energy. To remain a separate being after death, there must
exist the ability to maintain the structure of the radiant
body by the action of attention. This is why we have been
so insistent that you meditate. Otherwise, we will lose
you when you die and we don't want that. If a being cannot self-maintain after the elemental body no longer does
it automatically, it is absorbed into the flux of conscious
energy. You go into the light, as it were.

Isn't this going to heaven?
There is an element of ecstasy, but it is not complete.

When another elemental forms that fits the pattern of that particular fragment, it will return to the physical in search of more sensation. Or, if one never does, its unfulfilled desires will remain forever as a part of the tapestry of memory.

Would the person perceive this? Feel happy? Feel trapped?
These memories are somewhat self-aware. But they do not know themselves as beings. Just as your memory of your childhood games with Mike do not have a being of their own, but rather are part of a greater whole.

You remember my childhood?
I do, of course. But we will return to that later.

How does a person evolve this radiant body?
The imprinting of essence with experience requires effort and attention. It is the object of all "paths" and "ways" to higher consciousness. It is the object of real prayer. To begin, you must meditate. Who does not meditate, disintegrates.

Any specific recommendations?
Paying attention to physical sensation is paying attention to energetic sensation. Being awake to oneself and one's surroundings increases the intensity of the impressions

so that they affect the spin of the electrons that are present in the nervous system. In this context, being awake means being aware of one's own self while at the same time absorbing impressions from the outside. The increase in spin and enrichment of the complexity of the pattern of being that results brings more and more form to the radiant body. You will remember yourself after your death—who and what you were, why you existed, and what you intend for your future. You will, in short, acquire a true aim, and join the companions of God in their journey toward ecstatic and conscious union with one another and all that is. It is the difference between being a plant and being Rembrandt. The plant has a certain fragment of self-awareness, but Rembrandt is vastly complex, a being rich with fully realized talents and self-awareness that makes him a worthy companion in higher form.

Rembrandt was a saint?
Rembrandt was conscious. As far as his being a saint is concerned, though—forget it. Radiant being and sainthood are not the same thing, believe me.

So he persisted as a radiant being? Where is he now?
That's his business.

What about those who don't acquire this ethereal independence?
After death you cannot be blind and therefore you cannot change. There, you wait.

Wait for what?
To understand that, you must first understand that the living and the dead share the same world. Your dead are not off somewhere in space. Their lives and beings are intertwined with yours. They see all that passes here, but can only affect it indirectly, if they can make themselves heard in the minds of the living. However, you the living are changing now. As this change proceeds, you are better and better able to feel the presence of your dead. You will find your dead in the immediate surroundings of their lives, for the most part, clinging to what they can of their memories, attempting to preserve their selves despite the magnetic attraction of what would envelop them.

So the light is not our friend?
The light is the fate of sleeping man. Awakened man makes his own light, as part of the radiant choir who sing forever the song of God, which is the word.

But what about people from the distant past? Surely they don't linger here.
There is no other place for you to linger. If you are not an

independent being after death, you remain engaged in the life of the earth, awaiting your chance to recur and increase your being. Lives in elemental form change the patterns of the electrons that form the soul and intensify their spin. The great dead have lived lives consciously devoted to the evolution and growth of the radiant body. But most of you, in the state of death, bear only fragmentary bits of what you were in life. Simple patterns, weak spin, no clear form to the radiant body and no ability to maintain it. You are subject to a process of recurrence so powerful that there are none from the distant past, except the radiant.

How do we access past lives?
All may remember all. You do not realize what you are.

And what of death itself? What should we expect?
A death is as unique as a face. You die into your expectations. But you generally survive them.

Somebody who doesn't believe in the soul?
They make a great discovery.

So some become radiant bodies, some linger and try again, and some enter the memory of God? Who enters the memory of God?
Those who have no further potential and have not grown

into anything. But recall that their experience does not go anywhere. It dies with the elemental body because it is insufficiently potent to survive. What survives is generally nothing but a tiny essence, a spark that would be barely recognizable as the person who had previously existed.

What is essence?
Taste. The way a certain specific being tastes. Essence is foundation.

So the bad essences go back to God. God gets the dregs?
Every life is an experiment. Not all succeed. But most do, to enough of a degree that the being-body will remain coherent, clinging to the earth in the region of its memories. When a body is created that fits its essential attachments, it will be drawn to that body by a magnetism that it cannot resist. Birth to this world is death to the other, and vice versa. The recurrence is a great breathing.

What do these souls do while waiting?
They experience peace, some of them, only coming slowly into an awareness of what they need to continue on. Others are frantic, because of the nature of their lives. There can be great anguish, as loved ones are witnessed in the nakedness and, often, the horror of their own lives. There can be obsession, and the lusts of life can be end-

lessly indulged but never satisfied, for the physical world
can be seen but not touched by these beings. However,
there is also kindness among them. In a world where there
are no secrets, only truth, the compassion of one for another is very great.

Can the dead influence the living?
Not these little ones, not much. They have not the knowledge or wisdom to make themselves heard.

What are psychics?
A part of the electromagnetic field that fills the nervous
system rests a few centimeters above the skin, outside of
the body. This field is an organ just like the heart or the
brain. It is in quantum superposition, the electrons effectively everywhere in the universe and nowhere specific. It may be imprinted by information from anywhere
and any time. With it, you may see other worlds, you may
see the past and the future, you may see into the lives of
those around you. You may haunt God. However, the
process of imprinting itself causes the organ to cease to
be in superposition and thus to cease to be accessible to
further imprinting. In psychics, there is either an inborn
or learned ability to balance the attention in such a way
that these impressions do not cause this organ to become

focused into particulate form. The ability to control this organ can be developed.

How?
Many practices will work, but the best is to meditate in such a way that the mind is concentrated on physical sensation. This relieves the pressure of impressions incoming from the physical world on the electromagnetic body and enables it to expand.

How far can it expand?
Anybody can become God.

In life?
In life.

How can a mere imperfect human being become the master of the universe?
What is imperfect is your vision. You can find your perfection right now, this moment, always.

What is this seeing? This marvelous seeing you allude to?
You must understand the difference between sight and imagination. Real inner vision unfolds with an unmistakable spontaneousness. What is seen, also, is the same from

person to person. But the universe is so vast that only the most adept will be able to see the same thing one as another. It is even hard to go back to a place you have seen once before, unless there is a line of communication opened between yourself and somebody who is there.

This can become a scientifically valid means of communication?
It already is, even here. Although you do not presently understand the true meaning of indeterminacy, what you refer to as quantum physics offers a useful partial view of the inner workings of the physical world. Quantum instruments of communication, as your scientists now understand them, depend upon the entanglement of particles. You think now that you must separate two photons physically for them to be entangled, so your faster-than-light communications are limited by how far apart you can physically place the photons you entangle. But there was a time when all particles were in communication and so all are entangled. When you realize this, it will also be true that your quantum communications devices will be able to communicate instantaneously across all worlds. But until you realize it and understand it, it will not be true for you. Vision, in the manipulation of quantum reality, as in the perfecting of your being, is everything.

You seem to be referring to scientific progress and spiritual growth in the same breath.
They are the same. Your science progresses toward communication with all worlds only as fast as your spirit evolves. Animals may not leave their worlds, because they lack the ability to see the needs of others.

We are animals?
A true human being has four levels of mind. Most of you have only three, and perhaps a vestige of the fourth. Your destiny is to enter the humanity of the universe. But you may not fulfill it.

Are there such things as alien abductions?
As you grow in fourth mind, you see more.

Many of these encounters are brutal.
The kitten is terrified of the veterinarian. To subdue the little creature, violence is unavoidable.

But the slaughterhouse is also brutal.
Yours is not the destiny of the steer.

We aren't fodder for a higher world?
I know that you can ask clever questions. Don't try to play with me, Whitley.

That's an even more clever answer—what's your name, anyway?
If I said Michael?

An archangel in a turtleneck?
Legion, then?

*I think you're a perfectly ordinary person with an ordinary mother
and an ordinary name.*
I can imagine no greater honor than to be called human.

*Let me go back to the quantum issue, because I see that as some-
thing concrete that we can understand. You started by talking of
using superposition as a means of communication, then changed to
talking about entangled particles. What role does superposition
play in higher communication?*
The tiny layer of electrons that lies outside of the skin is
an organ in itself just like the eyes or the blood. It is a sen-
sory organ, but not one that operates naturally, except in
a few, as I have stated before. Even in them, it cannot be
used very effectively without higher consciousness. It is
the organ of higher consciousness. You must be able to
watch and not watch at the same time. When you learn
this, it will stay in superposition even as you take the imagery that it is receiving into your brain and process it.

You are speaking of opening the third eye?
The nervous system delivers these impressions to the area

of the brain closest to the pineal gland, which is where this organ is centered.

Can machines be created that "see," using an artificial version of this organ?

Machines are already being created that communicate via entangled photons. These machines will be the first that detect the voices of other worlds. It is also possible to create machines that mimic the action of the organ we have been discussing. But these machines must be conscious to work.

Conscious machines?

We will return to that later. There is a question lingering in your eyes that you have not asked. Ask it now.

You mentioned monsters in the world of the dead.

The acts of life affect the appearance of the dead in every tiny detail. Everything is imprinted upon the soul, often in surprising ways. Most dead appear as innocent children, longing for sensual lives and hoping that a body will be sparked that fits them. Some are aware enough of radiant being to try to ascend, but they always drift back, or if they become lost, are returned to earth.

By radiant beings?

Yes.

This creation of radiant bodies doesn't sound much like surrender.
On the contrary, it is total surrender. The unfocused fragments of lives barely lived do not contribute to the ecstasy
of God. God seeks true companions. Ecstasy is not ecstasy unless it is shared.

Can radiant bodies enter the physical world?
Radiant beings may be born into elemental bodies if they
wish, but these are acts of intention. Or it may be re-
quested that they do it, and they go on life-missions into
the elemental world. These can be dangerous missions
that cause them to fall from radiance, but also that may
greatly increase their ecstasy. So they go on these adven-
tures. It is happening a great deal now, which is why you
have so many glorious children among you. In addition to
entering the physical by means of being born, some high
beings may so perfectly create an image of the physical
bodies they once possessed that they can walk the streets.

Can they have babies?
This would be an act of God, but certainly it is possible.

Does it account for the birth of Jesus?
Jesus said that he was the son of man. Take him at his
word. He was God, though, a radiant body fully aware of
who he was and fully invested in all and everything. He

entered the elemental body consciously. But I remind you, all are God, all are Christ. The difference was that he knew it.

Was he a product of recurrence?
God is.

What of Jesus? What of Buddha?
Those are two different, but intertwined, questions. First, you must understand that the teachings of Buddha had reached the community of Hellenized Jews in which Jesus lived. So they form a part of Christianity. He was a spiritual revolutionary who brought a message of mercy and compassion and the dignity of man to a world of unimaginable terror. The Roman rule was blind and brutal and unspeakably greedy. Ancient knowledge was being murdered by Roman ignorance and Roman power. This knowledge consisted of how to consciously form a radiant body so that you would not recur into the physical, so that you would be free. Christ was here to preserve this knowledge and pass it down. But even his deposit was corrupted by Roman politicians, who transformed his practice into a religion after he died.

There was no resurrection, then?
No, that's just the point—there was. But you lost the un-

derstanding of it. The gospels describe what happened with great fidelity. He was seen. He did walk after his death. It was not his twin.

How?

His radiant body was under his conscious control. He could project an image of his physical body as he wished. Understand that there are practices of meditation and concentration also among the dead. When the angels sing, this is what they are doing, engaging in one of the disciplines of ecstasy. By releasing thought, they can themselves come into superposition, where they are not in any one place. Their consciousness can ride the infinite. They can see all worlds then, and participate in the ecstatic union that fills the universe. God will share all with all.

Could Christ appear again?

He has, many times, and Buddha. But remember that he comes as a thief, in the little shadows. His radiant body normally fills the cosmos, as I have explained, but it can be transformed into a form that is, in every respect, physical in appearance. The great error of the present is the way your religions externalize Christ. You are always calling on Christ. But you had better call on your own heart, for it is in your heart that his mansion is founded.

And Buddha?

He opened himself to the radiant world and gained its teaching, which he transmitted accurately. But let me re-phrase it in the terminology of this more informed age: the purpose of meditation is twofold. It is to organize the energetic body so that it will not lose its integrity after it can no longer depend upon the structure of the elemental body for its form. Then also, and in an interconnected manner, it is to fill the energetic body with objective sensation. Objective sensation is consciousness. You are within life, but not entirely absorbed in life. Part of you observes yourself from a distance. Remember this: if you do not watch, you do not see, and what you do not see does not impart any change in spin to the electrons that make up the energetic body. The parts of your life that you do not see are not carried with you into ecstasy, and it is ecstasy upon which the formation of the radiant body depends.

There are parts of my life that I would like to forget.

No. All life is potentially ecstatic, no matter what suffering or sin is involved. All life, child.

Why do we have elemental bodies?

They are essential to growth. The aim of mankind is to enter ecstasy. But to do this, you must be at once fully realized—that is, to carry with you into death all of your potential harvest of experience—and to be objectively conscious of this experience—not to be weighted with recriminations and regrets.

If we have hurt others in life, as we all have, then how can we ever be free of regret?
God forgives. But this does not mean that you should pray for forgiveness from some old graybeard in the sky. You must find who within you bears you forgiveness. An energetic body that bears such regrets bears them as areas of darkness, and if that body manifests its memory of its elemental self, the manifestation bears sores.

And we live again and again—why? What is the reason for recurrence?
To row the boat of being toward ecstasy. You must live many times in order to build up a radiant body that is complete. To be born into this world takes but an hour. But to be born into the next takes many lifetimes. Unless you follow your own real path, then you can do it more quickly. Remember this—path within, signposts without.

What are the signposts?
You find your own, in life, in love, in religion. But understand this: the teachings of Buddha, Christ and Muham-

mad are interlinked. They are one system in three, not three separate religions. This has been hidden from you for a long time.

Three in one? A triad?
A triad. Christianity is the active side of the triad, Islam the passive, Buddhism the reconciling. Christianity seeks God, Islam surrenders to God, Buddhism finds God. When you see these as three separate systems, you miss the great teaching of which each contains but a part. Seek the kingdom as a Christian, give yourself to God as a Muslim, find your new companion in the dynamic silence of Buddhist meditation.

Then a true seeker seeks in all faiths?
These three masters created one system. But there are many systems that have evolved in other ways, that have grown rather than been created.

Hinduism, for example?
The gods of the Hindus are the structures of personality purified into their essential meaning. Hinduism is the path of soul-knowledge, for knowledge of the gods is knowledge of the soul. The great systems of self-knowledge were the Egyptian religion and Hinduism. No amount of scientific knowledge of the "unconscious" will

provide as much food for the energetic body as true relationship with the Hindu gods.

Who were Muhammad and Buddha?
Exactly who history portrays them to have been. But to
understand what happened to them, you must understand
that your entire pantheon of deities is you. God is you.
The gods are you. Angels and demons are you. So it was
mankind who spoke to Muhammad in his cave. So also, to
Buddha under the Bhodi Tree, and to Christ in the desert.
Who do you think showed him the cities of the plain?
Satan is man, just as God is man. Satan seeks, God waits.
But you do not surrender. Not even Muslims. Although
the great Sufis have, some of them, somewhat, surrendered to God. As long as you defy God by self-will, Satan
finds you and captures you.

Why don't we surrender?
Self-will, the illusion that you can act and must act on
your own behalf, prevents you from entering the will of
God. And the God of which I speak is not a distant being off in some heaven. You yourself are the distant being
you seek.

But if the self is God—
No, please, listen. God is not this "self" of yours which

your western culture imagines. God is all being. To surrender to God is to make your energetic body transparent, so that the light of God shines through you. This "self" that so fascinates the west is only your brain-filtered concept of you as you appear to yourself in this life. It is very small. It does not include any of the experience you have amassed in other lives. Many human beings, at this point in history, are immense. But your concept of self is constricted. It relates only to this one life. It is tiny. The God within you is unimaginably vast.

You speak of a journey toward self-perfection. But isn't perfection impossible for us to achieve?
You can become perfect. Buddha did. Muhammad did. Christ did. Many have, hidden to history, done the same. You may find Buddha sleeping on a park bench, Muhammad pumping gasoline, Christ starving in the backstreet.

But if Christ was God, and God is perfect, why would he need to become perfect?
Christ was not perfect or he would not have been human. His humanity asked that the cup be taken from him, his divinity died a conscious death. But you must understand that his imperfect humanity and his perfect divinity were the same thing. That seems irreconcilable, but it isn't, because even when Christ suffered, he was in ecstasy. I am

here to get you to recognize yourself as divine—that is to say, as a participant in ecstasy even during elemental life. The new man will live in ecstasy, even though he lives in chains.

Define ecstasy.

The energetic body has a spin, or vibration. This can go infinitely fast. It can reach beyond the speed of light, and exit time altogether. When this happens, the body begins to radiate of its own accord. It becomes at once God and co-creative with God, a companion. A single bit of God, which you are, does not only join the whole like a crumb in a cake, it can attain so much of ecstasy that it becomes the whole. Your destiny, each of you, is to become all of God. But this process is slowed by contact with the points of attachment—and there are trillions and trillions of them—between the energetic and elemental bodies. So detachment, as Buddha said, is essential to ecstasy. The proper use of meditation is to enable you to see life as both an outsider and a participant. The outsider notices the glimmer of sunlight upon the spoon, the sensation of the food in the mouth, for he is using life to gain impressions. The participant only eats. So also, the outsider sees the packed bodies around him, he smells the sweat and the urine, he hears the soft clatter of the crystals with absolute objective calm, and inhales the searing torment of the gas without being in any way identified with the injustice or the cruelty or the terror all around him. But the participant screams, it suffers the agony of the elemental body, and knows the greatest terror man has ever known, which was experienced in the dark gas chambers of the Holocaust.

Are you dead?
Yes.

And did you die a Jew in the camps?
I died with each of them and all of them. When you kill a being, you kill all being. I die a million times a day. I am dying now, being murdered, being starved, devoured by bacteria, crushed, burned, shot, cut, slaughtered. But I am also being born, awakening into new life, playing in grass, discovering the hidden truths of nature, enjoying the sunshine, reading, eating, engaging in every sexual delight known, all now, all here, always.

And you are in ecstasy?
(He only gazed at me in answer.)

Then you are still here, a dead man among the living. You didn't leave when you ascended?
All leave, nobody leaves. Ascension is not a matter of fly-

ing off to some place in the sky, it is a matter of expanding
the being to fill the universe. You may ascend beyond time
and infinity, but you will still be here, as we all are.

Where is here?
Everywhere.

Ah. I'm lost.
All being includes all elements of the earth, and thus all
are part of all bodies. We are the consciousness of the
planetary level that it has spent all of its life evolving, each
and all of us. My being is the awakening earth. As is yours.
The destiny of earth and the destiny of man are one. If
we kill earth, we kill ourselves. If we die before our time,
then we will not be able to enter ecstasy as a whole being.
You are not a whole being, child. And "Whitley" is only a
tiny part of you. All mankind in all time is a whole being.

If we kill earth before we have all reached ecstasy, what happens?
We wait until and if the earth spins elemental bodies
once again that fit all the attachments of our energetic
bodies. If it does not, then we wait forever. We remain
incomplete.

What would this waiting be like?
Energetic bodies hunger to be radiant. They taste of ec-

stasy and want desperately to find their way to the completion of joy. But energetic bodies need return to time to reconstruct what of themselves impedes their ecstasy. If they cannot, they must suffer the anguish of regret and the pain of being able to see, but not enter, joy. When you taste of ecstasy, your hunger for more is appalling. It is *appalling*. It has driven me to wander the world, to construct this shell of flesh, to seek you out and come to you with my message, to serve you, little child, as my master.

What if earth never "spins" these new bodies?
We will join others in the same state. There are many.

We would be a species in hell, in effect?
We would be constantly aware that we had missed ecstasy. This pain I suffer now would last forever.

So the eternal joy of humankind depends upon the health of the earth?
Completely.

We think of ourselves as individuals. My sins are my own. My neighbor's sins are his problem.
Every joy, every sorrow, every good, every evil belongs to all. All are responsible for all. All are dependent upon all. Humanity is one.

But not all intelligent life. We are one species, but are there not others?
God is one. Ultimately, all being seeks to join all ecstasy. It is the destiny of every stone, every star, every intelligent creature and simple creature, to become the word. And the word, then, will be made flesh.

I don't understand. Hasn't that already happened?
It is always happening. But there will come a time when the stars themselves fall. The universe is breathing, expanding and contracting. It has happened many times before. Eventually, it will all contract to something no bigger than a baseball. Then it will explode again, journeying once more through the vastness. Each time it dies, though, it is reborn at a new and higher intensity. Eventually, there will come a moment when its rebirth is so energetic that the velocity of the "big bang" will exceed the speed of light. At that instant, the material world will, itself, go beyond time. Then the prophecy will be fulfilled, "I am."

And we are all part of God?
We are not part of God, we are God.

And all other species, what of them?
The tree, the worm, the wolf. All are God.

Worms are eternal beings?
Even the smallest spark unto itself is great.

Then the fly and the rat are ascended beings?
They cannot change. You can change. Look to your own soul.

God, then, is in the fragments?
God is like a hologram. The whole is fully present in every fragment, no matter how small.

So the whole of God is in the tip of my finger?
The whole of God is in a grain of sand. In a single electron. A quark.

I had not thought of God as a hologram before.
Infinite consciousness is in everything. In your pajama. In my sweater. All knowledge is present in every cell, every spark of fire, bit of trash.

That's—it's appalling.
The universe is the flesh of God.

But I have no access to the whole. I feel like a little fragment. I don't even know if I have a soul. And I certainly don't feel like part of God.
This is a fallen world and you are an imperfect being.

The essence of your imperfection is that you cannot see yourself as you are. Many lives must live before this will change. Mankind is a community of about ten billion fragments, and each must become transparent to the light of God before we, as a species, can journey on.

Earlier you seemed to imply that you were an alien. Then God. Now you're human. What are you?
Whatever you say.

A useful thing to be. How many human beings from earth have become radiant bodies?
About half.

Half! I thought it would be fifty or a hundred at most.
Humanity is a tremendous engine of the sacred. But among the living, there are only as many such beings present as absolutely essential for the welfare of the others.

How can we tell who's ascended and who isn't?
The meek shall inherit the earth. Understand this, and you will find them by what is in their hearts.

Who are the meek?
Those who are humble enough in self-will to surrender to higher will.

How can we tell if we are surrendered to higher will?
Go to the children. They will tell you with their eyes what you are.

Could we ever be rescued, if we destroy the earth before we were finished perfecting ourselves?
Nobody can change except inside the stream of time. Outside of it nothing changes. Nothing can. We enter the time stream by inserting our energetic bodies into elemental bodies on this planet of which we were born.

What about going to another planet?
The leaf cannot grow on another tree.

It can be grafted.
If you are given leave to enter the interstellar world in the elemental body, you will go as the others do, from a firm foundation of radiant being. But if you destroy your world, you die here.

We could travel the stars?
If you are good householders, you may participate in the life of the whole city of God. There exists a world now that is waiting for human help. Just as your world is being helped by others now.

What form does this help take?
It is a process of creating questions that can neither be borne nor answered. You know this.

I have written of it—evolutionary pressure. It explains what's being done to us—the theatrical appearance of UFOs in the sky, the assaults on us by night, the ferocious official secrecy, the collapse of the environment—all of it.
It is all part of the plan of your evolution. Pisces, the little fish, will be poured out onto dry land by the stream of Aquarius. Then, how will you live? How will you breathe? You will make a leap of evolution. You will square the circle or die.

Now what about this other world you mentioned, waiting for our help?
You will be the aliens one day, to these others. Bear in mind that, if you do not survive, then they will never receive your help. Your welfare is essential to theirs, just as you depended, without knowing it, upon those who are here for you.

Have you traveled to other worlds?
I belong to many worlds.

Are you from another planet that is like ours?
I am human.

What's it like, going to another planet?
Other worlds exist on many different levels, and contain beings of many different levels and appearances. The details from world to world can be very different. But the basic laws of reality remain the same.

Which is why the visitors communicate with me in Masonic terms? Precisely. Three is three and seven is seven. The craft is God's plan for freedom.

You are endorsing Masonry?
I am endorsing the craft in its most impeccable form. Where the craft is secret, there is danger of corruption.

It's become a charitable and social group in the United States.
Not entirely.

Why is it secret?
It was the government of the world in early times. But the world fell. After humanity ceased to be surrendered to the law of God, the craft had to become secret in order to stay alive.

How do you travel to other planets?
You must learn to manipulate mass.

Manipulate mass?
The mass of bodies can be controlled by those who know
the secret.

Will we learn it?
When it is time, all will come to you. But remember, it is
you who will choose the time. You exist on many levels,
the living in their levels and the dead in their levels. Man
is governed from the radiant level.

*But our world is dying and falling into chaos? How can we be
governed poorly from such a high level?*
Man is a child. Children govern children with the wisdom
of children.

There are aliens here?
Using you and guiding you.

We're being exploited?
You are, but also helped. You are being guided to your
place as guides of another world.

What will we do for this other world?
You will draw it toward ecstasy just as your mentors draw
you toward ecstasy. Right now, there are brilliant crea-

tures there looking at the sky and devouring the flesh of their own children, just as you did. Unless you help them, they will not make their evolutionary leap in time, and will go extinct.

Whose responsibility would that be?
All are responsible for all.

How many worlds are there like ours, like theirs?
The planets that can sustain complex elemental bodies are not many. However, the elements of which they are made occur in various patterns, and the form of evolution depends upon the chemical makeup of the planet upon which it occurs. So there are worlds where creatures look very much like us. There are worlds where they are quite different.

Could aliens walk among us without our noticing?
By bending light, they can be invisible, and walk here to some extent, and also by using means to prevent you from looking at them by influencing your mind from a distance. But there are also those patterned on the same template as you, and they walk freely here. It is their job to enforce secrecy. This is the source of all the confusion about this. They appear, for example, to be part of your

government, but they only use it as camouflage and as
a source of power. Human institutions do not control the
secrecy. It is controlled from a higher level.

Are you on that level?
Yes.

Another world is in control of this one?
Yes.

What about all the horrors that happen here?
Remember that man has two sides, light and dark. To see
the light, you must bear the darkness.

How do they control this world?
By planning, and they use mind control.

Am I under mind control?
The opposite. The technological intervention that has
occurred in your case has been done to make certain that
general fields of control will not affect you.

General fields of control?
Directional suggestion that is applied to all who are en-
hanced electrically. This is the means of control of mili-
tary and government.

Telepathy?
Radio frequencies. Extremely sensitive circuits can pick up and decode thought. Microwaves can be used to project thought into the brain. But the fields of which I speak are much more general. They create tendencies. The desire is to preserve the maximum amount of freedom in the maximum number of individuals.

Have any people from earth ever gone to other worlds?
A whole world of human beings has been evolved artificially off the planet, and they come and go freely.

What are you talking about?
Human beings are being born and raised off the earth. You can find their habitations if you look. They live in this solar system.

My God. How many?
Thousands.

What do they do here?
They enforce mankind's blindness by preventing science from exploring the key mysteries of the past and discovering a practical means of expanding into the universe, and they maintain the official secrecy that keeps the question of whether or not aliens are here from being answered.

Why do they harm us so terribly?
The objective of resistance is to make you strong. The weight lifter puts more and more weight to himself, so that he'll be able to lift more and more.

If he puts too much?
He breaks his back. He fails by overreaching himself.

Or his trainer fails him by pressing him to do more than he is able.
Then he was not meant to be a champion, and we know that is not true of mankind. Mankind is meant to ascend.

Will we ever be strong enough?
Surrender to God and your enemies will become your friends.

What is being done to us? What was done to me?
The body of man is being altered so that the barrier that presently prevents you from knowing one another's thoughts will fall. You are being put under pressure in order to increase the speed of your evolution. An attempt is being made to induce an evolutionary leap. Only desperation will do this. There will come a time when your planet is dying and you are dying, and you will see these aliens all around you. But they will not help you, no

matter how hard you beg, and you will beg, believe me. Their inaction, however, is their help. As agonizing as it is for them to see you suffer, they do it out of compassion, for without it you will not succeed in the mission of this age, which is to open the elemental body to ecstasy. Mankind, over the next two thousand years, is destined either to go extinct or ascend. The elemental body will become transparent to the radiant body, which will shine with the light of God.

So how are we to approach God? What is the nature of this infinite being that resides in every grain of sand?
When you say God, you think of somebody outside of yourself. You think as the age of worship thinks. Over the last age, that of Pisces, the elemental body was changed by this process of worship. It is not the same as it was two thousand years ago. Now the receptacle is larger. Now each of you can contain all of the universe. That was not true then. Now this is a species of sacred beings. But you are babies, and so still ignorant of your powers. The last age was the age of the external God. This is the age of God within.

What about our religions? Do they offer us a path back to God?
You have no religions. Religions don't have victims. There is a new path.

What is it?

Religion must be brought inside you. No longer look to gods without, look to God within. Unless you bear the kingdom within you, the kingdom will perish from the earth, and if that happens, there will be long ages of darkness and suffering, at the end of which man will once again be only an intelligent animal. You will lose everything, every trace of memory, of history, science, technology, mathematics, all of it. If you do not find the kingdom, human consciousness will die. You will revert to your animal nature, which is already happening all around you. People who are debased have lost their humanity. They have become brilliant animals.

Why do our religions have victims?

Because they demand belief, and belief is always a lie, for the essence of reality is not fact but question. There are no facts, only truths. So love of God has nothing to do with belief. Belief rejects God. Communion with God is a science, the science of self-discovery and self-knowledge. Among you, though, this is a lost science, the science of faith.

How can we regain it? Is something like the Eucharist part of this science?

Christ gave the Eucharist to mankind. But the Eucharistic

feast was enacted from time immemorial. It began when you still lived in the forest. When the strong died, you ate their flesh to gain their strength.

Did it work?
Don't joke with me. It was pitiful.

Is there a record of the Eucharist before Christ?
There is.

What is it?
I'm not interested in answering. You will find the science of ascension in the dancing of the Sufis, the meditations of the Yogi, the prayer of the Christian monastics. This science is lost as a science, but it can be regained.

Was Christ God?
The promise of resurrection is the essential promise of being. Rebirth is not a literal reconstitution of the elemental body. It is, rather, awakening from the sleep of being. Resurrection can take place in you right now. You are Lazarus in the tomb, all of you. And Christ is always knocking upon the door, calling you to come out. Soon, the tomb will be torn down around you, and you must come out.

Did Christ rise?
Most die by nature. Christ died by intention.

What is the process of resurrection?
The energetic body detaches from the elemental body
when it can no longer sustain its attachments. Christ's
energetic body was radiant. But it left its elemental body
just like yours will and everybody's does. The work of the
demon among you is to deceive you into believing that
Christ was better than you. Christ said it: I am the son of
man. Christ is all. All are Christ.

What about the ancient faiths? Wicca, for example?
Modern Wicca is not an ancient faith. It is a new faith
that recognizes an ancient practice. The earth is worthy
of worship, for it gave you all that you are and have. It
offers an impeccable path.

What religion doesn't offer an impeccable path?
Hidden in the ruins are diamonds. Remember, a diamond
is forever. *(Laughs.)*

*But what about the rebirth of the body? This is a powerful strain
in our religious traditions, that the body will rise again.*
It is a memory from the last civilization that the ignorance
of the survivors has drawn into myth. The simple people

were allowed to know nothing of science in that age, and so they saw its action as a miracle and thought that the dead were being made to rise. But the science of the soul is just another science. There is no supernatural, only physics. But the physics and electronics involved in communicating with intelligent energy is very subtle. Nothing, however, that you are not capable of now. The devices needed to make your beginning are already sold in stores.

What devices do you refer to?
Devices that detect magnetic fields and electromagnetic plasmas. You will find living energetic beings in this way. They will not be very richly alive, but they will be there. You may also detect simple energetic beings that have little intelligence. They are all around you.

What do we do once we've detected them?
Then you must be physically able to communicate. After a time, you will not need instruments to detect them, once you become attuned to their presence around you. But don't expect them to offer you endless wisdom. Many of the dead who wait in the world have less than you do, by a very great deal. But not all. Some are exceedingly rich, and can report to you even about the true past and the logical future, and can share themselves with you in ways that you can hardly imagine now.

What practice would make us physically able to communicate?
Over the course of our discussion, everything you need to
learn how to objectively communicate with these beings
will be given, just as all information necessary for your
science to begin to detect living energy, which is trying
now to communicate with you.

How?
An example would be the much maligned crop circles.
These are two-dimensional portraits of these beings,
self-created. They are trying to introduce themselves to
this age.

The crop circles are not hoaxes?
No.

Why doesn't anybody believe in them?
To face the return of the dead is to face the change of the
age. For those souls who are yet incomplete, this is terri-
fying, because they fear two things: first, that this por-
tends that the time during which they can grow and
develop is ending; second, that they will, if they conjoin
the world of the dead, also see as the dead see, and thus
become unable to change even if the earth remains able
to support elemental bodies. So they pretend that it's all

false. There are many other reasons to conceal such things, but these are the strongest.

What has this all got to do with resurrection?
The resurrected man is a consistent theme of the mythology that developed out of observations of a certain type of being, beginning with Osiris and ending with Christ. Fully conscious beings adept in this science can enable the radiant body to appear as an elemental body, so perfectly imprinted are its sensations on their energetic being.

Is your body, right now, radiant?
You look for facts in a place where there is only truth. All bodies are one body.

But I thought you said that the elemental and energetic bodies were separate, and that the energetic body could become radiant, which I take to mean self-sustaining.
The radiant body is the part of you that is conscious in the energetic world. It is in every cell of the elemental body, and indeed, is its life. There is nothing mysterious about the soul, or even about its eternal life. Energy is eternal, so the part of you that is energy is eternal. What has been hard for you to understand is that the speed at which these electrons move carries the taste of your being

and the memory of your lives. Each one carries a different fraction of the whole. There are trillions of electrons in a single elemental body, and they contain a detailed memory of every second of life. This is why, for example, when certain areas of the brain are probed, the physical buffering mechanism can be paralyzed, causing the memories stored in this way to flood into the chemical cells. The person then has stunningly detailed recall of past events, as if the moments were being lived again. Nothing of your life is forgotten, or of all your lives. When you are dead, you are your whole self, in every detail. You know yourself entirely. The things about yourself that you cannot bear and suppress now are entirely and completely present to you and to all others. The dead have no privacy, and the living have no privacy from them. The dead see everything that you do. It is part of their task to bear the errors and enjoy the triumphs of the living.

What is real religion?
From outside of time, man's effort to know God appears as a single form, a work of art that has evolved across history. You have created it in three phases. The first is negative, the age of sacrifice. This is why the Old Testament God is so terrible. The moment that God tells Abraham not to kill Isaac is a record of one of the most sacred of all human moments, for it sets the stage for the next age.

The second age is positive, the age of worship. This is why the God of the New Testament is full of compassion. Your present age is when man and God become one. You find in yourself Christ, Buddha, Allah, Krishna. In this age, the elemental body has evolved to the point that it has the potential to reflect divine ecstasy. It is happening already, in the secret lives of your own children. I am here to bring you a promise from on high: if you surrender yourselves to God, you and the earth will be saved. Otherwise, you will be extinct before the end of the age.

You describe our historical effort to know God as a work of art. What do you mean?

You are weaving a tapestry of living memories. This is what the body of man is—a great weave of shimmering, living cloth. It is full of all the hopes, failures, fears and attainments of the ages. Every detail is there, every step taken by every foot upon every path, not just the acts of Buddha or Christ or the great leaders. Nothing has been forgotten, not the single drawing of a single breath. All lives are all completely present in this work of art.

What about the gas chambers? Are they part of it?

High deliverance has a dark foundation. There were extraordinary instances of resurrection in those terrible places. Life was lived at transformational intensity during the gassing. They transformed the evil of their deaths into the glory of God. Those who died with rage and terror in their hearts also died with courage and compassion in their hearts. God was their rabbi.

But if there had been no gas chambers, would there then have been none of this grandeur?

They made of their suffering, with great effort, what one who attains the heart of a child may easily make of the drift of a cloud or the peaceful ringing of a bell upon a summer evening. And only a few. Most died in agony and confusion, all for nothing. It is easier to reach ecstasy through joy than through suffering.

What happened to the Nazis?

It takes great courage to enter an elemental body, because you are putting yourself in a position where the weakest part of you may imprint your energetic body eternally. Sin is that which bars us from ecstasy. How does sin actually feel after death? At first, after you die, you begin to taste of the most exquisite pleasure. It is extremely intimate, extremely personal, and as it builds, you begin to live in more and more of your lives. You taste the food and smell the air, you kiss your kisses and love your loves, and it gets more and more beautiful and more and more innocent. And then, suddenly, your hand is opening the gas canister—and you are swept with all the fear that made you do it, the primitive tribalism that you indulged to monstrous and distorted proportions. You feel sick with a filthy disease, you feel agonizingly ugly, as you kneel at the feet of those you destroyed. And they see you, utterly, as you are. They glow with compassion for you, but their compassion causes you the most terrible anguish because of what it makes you see, and you fall back from ecstasy. You cannot bear to be seen or to see the glory around you, which seems to you like a searing fire, so you turn inward, shielding yourself as a man would shield himself from the burning sun. But you cannot escape. For you, the fire of ecstasy is the fire of agony.

What about little sins?
Little imperfections are simply part of nature. Sin is willful indulgence of imperfection. Most sin is hidden during life. You have sins. I can see them. But you hide them from yourself.

What are my sins?
Living among you, as I do, is to live in an ocean of sacred beings who have no idea what they are. The man in

the room next to this sleeps a troubled sleep, but I see
the glory of his radiant body, and the couple above, who
are engaging in fellatio, I see her patient faith in deliverance, and in him, I see a brave heart on a journey to glory.
But I also see the way they see themselves, the shadows
of their recriminations and disappointments. Be as little
children.

*I realize that you see us all totally, and I must say that you've
caught me by surprise.*
(Laughs) Watch out for the thief.

What will happen to me?
To die takes great courage. This is the glory of the living world, its courage. For, after all, most of you have no
knowledge of higher worlds at all. They cannot feel their
energetic body. They die as they live, blind. But you are
not blind.

What about my wife and son?
They will suffer and die, as all. I will pray for them, that
they may find joy in the transit of their lives.

You'll pray for them?
Is that so strange?

Because you'd be praying to yourself. I think you're God.
I think you're God.

What is real religion?
A means of transforming accident into fate. It is a science.
Real religion and real science are the same.

I don't understand.
Fate is life lived. Accident is life let pass. To live means
to notice and take responsibility. Otherwise, it just happens as it happens. Because you are fallen, you cannot see
the difference between the large-scale aim of being and
the randomness of chance. To be fallen is to be blind.
This is the land of the blind.

Can we be cured of our blindness?
Let me offer you a picture of the universe as it really is.
There are many thousands of worlds like this one, in vary-
ing states of development. Some are worse off than yours,
others better. Some have even reached such ecstasy in the
elemental body that they can enjoy congress across the
reaches of space and time. In these worlds, the elemental body is radiant. The physics of material being for
them is the same as the physics of energetic being. This
is why, when they come among you, they may walk through

walls, or fly, or disappear or change form. But most beings
in other worlds live and die confined to the planets of
their origin, as you do.

*You said thousands of worlds. I would have thought millions—
billions.*

Intelligent life is extremely rare because planets which
can sustain complex bodies are extremely rare. Life, however, is common. It is not just planetary. Life is ubiquitous. It is a part of the essential structure of reality—the
nervous system, as it were, of the body of God. There is
much energetic life, for example, that is not intelligent.
Life need not be planet-bound at all.

Why is life so common?

Because perception is essential to the structure of the
universe. If a thing is not perceived, it doesn't have form.
Life is thus the mechanism that gives form to nature.
However, matter need not be perceived by an intelligent
creature to have form. When it is, different laws apply,
because the perception of intelligent creatures influences
the form of what they perceive by the expectations built
into their brains. The universe looks as it does to you, and
functions by the laws that you see controlling it, because
of the way your brain manages the process of perception.
Conscious creatures, however, may control the form of

the universe. The truly conscious are responsible for the laws that intelligent creatures follow by nature.

Will we ever be conscious?
If you survive.

What is consciousness?
Self-realization. A fully self-realized being understands the whole creation, for it is completely present everywhere.

I could understand everything?
Not in your current state of being. You can only understand as much as the structures of your elemental body can support. But you understand only a small part even of that.

How far away from understanding all that I can now understand am I?
If all you could understand in your present state was a star the size of the sun, then your understanding right now is a thimbleful of light.

Well, that isn't much.
On the contrary, it is a very great deal. You human beings are right on the edge of becoming a conscious species.

This is why we are here. We're midwives to your birth, as you yourself have speculated. You were to be born into consciousness before, but you miscarried. You fell from understanding because you misused the power that your growing consciousness gave you. Better to start over again.

How did we misuse this power?
In those days, there were a few people on the earth with understanding greater than that of all your great scientists of today. But they guarded their knowledge ferociously. They were extremely secretive. The average man was little more than an animal, eating his brother for strength. So they lost everything, because you are a single being, and thus only as conscious as the least of you.

Theirs was a slave state?
Your world is a slave state. You are all slaves to the demons who run it, who keep you in ignorance.

Our leaders are demons?
They wish to conceal real knowledge from the common man, just as was true in the past civilization. Secrecy destroyed that world, and, if this one is to die, it is secrecy that will destroy it. This is why they conceal the truth about the past and the presence of those who seek to help you. They think that they do this on behalf of mankind,

some of them, but they actually seek the destruction of the species. This hunger for self-destruction is the essence of your dark side, but we will speak of the death wish later. If you passively let them confine the wealth and keep the secrets, I will overturn your world yet again.

You could personally destroy our entire world?
(Silence.)

Name some of these demons.
Find the demon in your own heart, then I will betray the demon rulers of your world to you. Remember that the evil also serve me. Without evil, you could not taste of the good. Without them, you could not make the choice to follow me.

But a moment ago you said that aliens were here actively suppressing our progress. Now you say it's our leaders. What does this mean?
You must take your future from the hands of your oppressors. Do you think that there is a single human heart that is not filled with love for mankind? No, your demons make you strong.

Who are you? Christ? Or a demon yourself?
Stop thinking this way. This is no longer the Middle Ages.

Be objective. Remember that God is in everything. The whole of creation is the matter of God. Nothing is separate from God, nor can ever be. Your sense of independence is an illusion, so that you can take the journey of discovery. So also, no matter what you may call me, I am in God.

But what about the people who keep the secrets, for example, about aliens? Or the secrets about the past as it really was, or conceal the truth about Mars?

When they die, they will see that they have crystallized imperfections in themselves by the indulgence of self-will. They will suffer the fire of love, as I have already described it. Some of them will die in eternity and be part of you no more. Others will go on to become companions of God.

What about me?

You know what you are. Don't ask me.

You are saying that the demon is not evil, that he is—what—the bringer of knowledge?

We learn from our mistakes. But those who give themselves to evil suffer. Make no mistake. They can become so heavy that they sink into the earth. Just as the energetic body can enjoy extraordinary pleasure, it can suffer excruciating pain. You have in your body a few million nerves. But in your energetic body, every tiny bit of being can experience the totality of ecstasy or agony.

There are those who experience eternal agony?
A fallen master may, one who by some foolish intention rejects the joy of the kingdom. But remember, always, that were it not for the darkness of the night, you would not see the stars. Look into your astrophysics texts. You will find that your science does not understand the darkness. The darkness is the compassion of God, which gives us our vision of the universe. So also, the darkness in your heart is your own compassion toward yourself, for unless you bore evil, you would not be able to discern good.

This suggests to me that the fall of man has to do with a mistake of some kind. We failed to understand something. What did we fail to understand?
That the kingdom of heaven is within you. Not one human being, living or dead, has ever been able to face that, not since it was uttered. But if you cannot find the kingdom, you cannot gain the kingdom.

How can we regain our vision?
Fear is blindness. Fear rules this world. It is extremely deep. When a microbe is threatened, it will recoil. That's how deep fear is. In the fields, fear rides. In the struggle

of the deer to survive the jaw of the wolf or gunfire of
the man, fear rides. A shadow has fallen here, into the
very atoms that construct this place.

This is an impossible problem. It's beyond our ability to correct.
If one of you could live one moment without fear, then
all the world would be free. The emergence of physical life is at once its fall and its salvation. How can you
be fallen and ascended at the same time? In other words,
how may the elemental world gain communion with the
energetic one? The hidden meaning of mankind is that
you may reconcile the irreconcilable. You are here to save
all that lives on earth from the fear of death by surrender-
ing your will to God's. Read the Koran, listen to Muhammad. He brought the message of surrender impeccably.
You say that it is impossible. It is. But you are here to
square the circle. This is why earth evolved intelligence.
The aim of mankind is to clear the vision of the living,
so that you can join in full consciousness to the dead, and
thus learn that fear of death is fear of nothing.

*There seems to be something very extraordinary hidden in what
you're saying. You're saying that the fall of mankind was the emergence of life on earth. Am I right?*
You are, but that is a three-dimensional view, and thus
limited by the limits of three-dimensional vision. Re-

member the analogy of how the two-dimensional being sees a solid object. As a ball passes through the flat plane on which such a being would be confined, it would not see the real shape, or even be able to conceive of it. By definition, a two-dimensional being cannot look up, for then it would see into the third dimension, which is impossible for it to do. What it would see, always looking straight ahead, would be a dot that would grow into a line, then slowly contract again into a dot and disappear. It would *never* understand the true nature of the ball, because its two-dimensional mind cannot contain the concept of a solid object.

I don't want to seem thickheaded, but I don't think you answered my question.
The inference should be enough.

It isn't!
The emergence of life on earth and the fall of man are the same, in two ways. First, outside of time, all events are one, so they happen simultaneously. Not that they have happened, but that they are always happening. Every moment is forever, as you will recall after you die and begin to live in your memories. You will see the importance, then, of living a life that satisfies you and fulfills your destiny, because everything you have done will be immediately

present in your consciousness all the time. Second, the emergence of the word—that is to say, the possibility of all things that may exist in concrete form—into physical reality placed it in the position of needing to struggle to survive. When the word became flesh, it became vulnerable. If physical beings don't struggle, you die. So you cannot surrender. And yet you cannot stop your fall unless you do surrender. If you continue to struggle against nature, you will die. But if you don't struggle, you will die. This is tragedy of the word in physical form, and is the essential human problem. This is the problem you must solve, if you are to avoid going extinct.

I think that's the most profound statement I've ever heard. You are defining the word as God manifesting into physical reality and thus including physical vulnerability and weakness in his perfection. I see this as the key to our salvation. Am I right?
The word is potential. Just as your uttering of the word "automobile" is not an automobile, but contains the possibility of one, so also this word contained the possibility of everything. The word was not God. The word was an idea that turned into sound when it penetrated the physical.

I'm disappointed. I saw more in what you said than was there.
No, you saw exactly, and your observation was precisely correct. But I want you never to forget that there is no

world but this one. The radiant world is not separate. It's all around you. Energetic being is just as detectable and accessible to science as elemental being.

God can be measured by science?
If you dare.

If we dare? What's to dare?
If you develop a means that will enable you to communicate with your dead, which, as I have said, is quite possible, you will begin to know, in life, what you are only meant to know in death. But the unready souls fear this congress. It is also why you tell yourselves that the soul is on some strange ethereal plane far distant from you. You fear to find it, because then you will have to face yourselves as you are.

Are we so terrible?
You are not terrible. Your fear is terrible. Instinct makes you fear congress with the dead, because they see more than you dare to see.

What did the word sound like?
I don't know, I wasn't there.

But what will actually happen to us? Will we return to the forest?
The civilization of the northern peoples will be reduced

to shadows and memories in the minds of the living. It will follow its own past because of its flaws.

What are its flaws?
Greed and secretiveness. All who keep secrets that others should know keep evil in their hearts. All who amass more than they need, take bread from others. The wealth of the first world is its sin, and it will go the way of sinful things.

What are good and evil?
They are teaching tools. You are free to embrace either, because in life you can be blind to the consequences. This blindness is your free will. It is what enables you to learn. If you could see as I see, you would never in a million years perform the least evil act. Never! But then, I've been along that road already.

Are you perfect?
God is.

I feel worshipful toward you.
Worship at your own feet. It is far more challenging to face your mastery.

I have no mastery.
That is your mastery.

What did you mean when you said our civilization would follow its own past?

What was here before you was very great. It uncovered the secret to which you are blind, the secret of communion with the dead. It began to be able to use intelligent energy in its technology. To use souls as tools. Look at the carvings at Dendera in Egypt. Those strange objects in the containers are not electrical filaments or religious symbols. Those are souls. The walls of the containers bear an electrical charge of a type that imprisons them. Because of the use of such technology, elemental bodies extended their perception outside of the time stream, with the result that the school of the earth ceased to work as a place of change. Who knows the truth, cannot find their weakness, and that is your aim on earth. What was worse, the knowledge of this power was kept from the common, ordinary people who have little self-will to begin with, and so are the only ones really capable of making good use of such abilities. The old world was destroyed because of its own greed and secretiveness. Those least evolved rose to the top, as happens here. Your leaders, as you call them, are all people with damaged senses of self-worth. The damaged goods run the civilization. That's why it cannot last.

Abraham Lincoln was damaged goods?
The need to lead is a symptom.

So Lincoln and Washington were no better than Hitler and Stalin?

Don't be childish. You know that not to be true. Great men have symptoms, too.

So what happened to the old world, as you call it—this civilization in which I'm not even sure I believe?

You lived in it—as, when you die, you will recall. It was destroyed and all of its works were undone and laid waste. Where there are now deserts, there were great cities. The very climate of the planet was changed, to make certain that the sands and the waters would forever cover the remains of your glory. Now your souls recycle again and again through life after life, returning each time stripped of all past memories, so that you would live each time as if you had never lived at all. This is why you and your world are called "Dead Forever."

Who calls us that?

God.

God dislikes us?

God is angry at you, but also in love with you. We are impatient for you to join the rest of us.

"Dead Forever" implies that God has a long time to wait.

The impatient must be patient.

What was this civilization?

You lost the thread. There was a war. Now the victors call earth "Dead Forever" because you are required to recur in the body until you are truly free. The wheel of life, as it is called by the Buddhists, is your prison.

The human soul is imprisoned?

It is imprisoned.

And nobody ever leaves the recurrence? Every soul eventually comes back for a new life?

All recur, all do not.

Will this ever end?

Your enemy does not want it to end. They fear you too much. When you see UFOs, you see prison guards. They also act within your society to confuse you about your own past, and to prevent progress in areas such as propulsion, which might enable you to spread into the heavens. This is all done to prevent you from escaping.

I thought the Holocaust was what prevented us from making progress leaving the planet.

I am speaking now of what is behind the evil done in your world—the large-scale, historical evil.

Who is this enemy?
You know them by many names. But you yourself had the
privilege of meeting your enemy face-to-face.

Was I in the company of demons or aliens on that night in 1985?
Remember that the air is never so sweet, nor thy wife so
comely, nor thy child so beautiful, as after the battle won.
We depend upon our enemy for the sweetness of our
lives. Love your enemy, for he is your best friend. Without the darkness, you would never know the glory of the
firmament.

*We are in chains, just as you said. But you also said you had
the key.*
This whole conversation is the key. You should bless your
jailers, because without them you could never find your
freedom. When you, as a species, remember why you have
been imprisoned, and you face what you did, you will
be free.

What did we do?
I can tell you plainly. But you will not believe me, not in
your hearts. Your hearts are in denial. Listen well, because
this is the first time the true story of the taking of the
fruit of the tree of knowledge has been said since you left
the garden. You went to war against God. You fought the

deepest meaning of the universe, in quest of what you thought you were missing. Greed drove you to seek this knowledge, which is knowledge of yourselves separate from God. You imagined that being surrendered to God was being enslaved by God. You did not see giving oneself to us is the only true freedom. It is not that man is the servant of God, but that man is God, as are we all.

There was an actual, physical battle?
There is a sacred science. It enables complete mastery of time and space. You had access to this science and used technology based on it. You went to war. This whole solar system bears scars from the battle, some of them terrible. You remember this, because you fought.

I don't remember a thing.
Your species bears a wound in its soul that makes you deny the reality of the past that is plainly visible all around you. Mars was murdered by you. At that point, intervention occurred, as it will again when you destroy this planet, as will probably happen. This is the trigger for intervention, the destruction of a living world.

Who intervenes?
God acts.

That is to say, you.

Remember that God is holographic. Thus all act when God acts. You act.

We remember this as the angel with the fiery sword who drove us from the garden?

The planet was seized with upheaval, its climate revised. You fought each other like starving rats, in the end. Then, when you had lost everything, your beautiful world was turned under by the hoe of forgetfulness.

And we lost access to the science of God—your science?

The part of your brain that enables you to utilize electrons without drawing them into the particulate state was turned off. You became time-bound. You went to sleep, sinking into the time stream, which is where you remain trapped.

What's going to happen to us?

You have come to the end of the resources that were given you in the time that was given you. We measured the rate at which you would expand and grow very precisely, and fitted your development to a calendar which we devised called the Zodiac. In your writings, Whitley, you have wondered why mankind would have such a long-count calendar. Why were simple farmers in need of it? They were not. We needed it. The constellations of the Zodiac are arbitrary inventions to enable us to mark the progress of the equinox and keep track of exactly where you are in your journey. At this moment, the little fish of Pisces is about to be spilled out onto the dry land by Aquarius. All you know how to do, little fish, is swim. How will you swim upon the dry land?

When you say "we," who do you mean? You have not made this clear.
In the Hindu tradition there is this story: The God of the Universe became curious about how it felt to be a pig. So he entered the body of one. He found it delightful beyond compare—how good the sty smelled, how sweet were the slops, how desirable were the female pigs. But the universe needed tending. There was work to be done. So the helpers and handmaidens went and said, "God, you must come out of there. The universe needs you." God said, "Who are you talking to? I am just a pig! Leave me alone!" So they killed the pig, and God came out, and refused to believe he had ever refused to leave.

And we're the pig?
Earth is the pig. You are its inhabitant.

You are responsible, then, for the destruction of mankind?
Yes.

How do you intend to do it?
We are doing it with wealth.

Please explain.
What you refer to as "the consumer society" is actually a mechanism designed to ensure your proper transition from Pisces to Aquarius. Each transition has such a mechanism. The last one, transferring you from Aries to Pisces, was the idea of the risen man. This idea, and the ethics of the gospel, gave you a structure upon which could be built a new society. But that time is past. The society has outlived its usefulness. It's time for something new. This is why the present mechanism is destructive, not constructive.

The consumer society is destroying the planet. And that's intentional?
After the suffering you are about to endure, mankind will never again lust after material wealth. You are about to suffocate in your own garbage.

You are talking about the death of billions in a sea of human agony. And you dare to set yourself up as a moral authority? What you're doing makes the Holocaust look innocent.
You are doing it. Your greed is the culprit.

I thought you were an angel.
You flatter me. I'm only a Canadian. But I don't pay taxes.

Do you have a driver's license?
No.

Do you have a home?
My home is within you.

Then this is a dream after all?
If you wish.

You seem real.
Appearances can be deceiving, as you will find when the end comes.

When will that be?
Look to the details of the transition between signs, and you will be able to find precisely where the earth will cease to support you.

Can you give me any more information?
It's all around you.

What is going to happen?
You've already been told.

Can we talk about God again? There's still something missing.
There is something missing in all of us.

What does that mean?
The question you asked is its own answer. What is absent within, is God. When you ask the question, "Who am I?" you can't really answer. Nobody can. The answer is God.

That's incredible.
How so? Do you fail to understand?

No, I do understand. That's what's so incredible. I didn't think a human being could understand this.
This is the first time this message is given.

Not even in that lost civilization you were talking about?
They did not understand who they were. That's why they were lost.

Can the soul be destroyed?
An atomic explosion throws all plasmas into chaos. They can also destroy themselves, and technological intervention may destroy them. Souls may last forever, but they may be exploited, even killed. They may be executed.

How can they be exploited?
Material of souls is harvested and used to make intelligent machines. An intelligent machine is a being without the potential to be free. In this sense, it is not alive. It must act as it acts.

Then why does it need to be intelligent?
An intelligent machine is insightful and precise.

Is it a terrible thing to exploit consciousness in this way?
Part of the reason that your species guards its soul-blindness so ferociously is a fear you hide from yourselves. It is the fear that you will not be able to cope with the fantastically powerful technologies that involve the use of souls. You failed in the past, and it marked you.

What is evil?
Entropy is the natural tendency of all things to disintegrate. Evil is the addition of intention to that process. Hate is like cold. It has an end. Love is like heat. It does not.

Do we all share in the production and reconstruction of souls?
Souls can do more than regret. There can be so much loathing that they commit suicide. They do this by isolat-

ing themselves from the greater whole, by seeking toward chaos.

Is there a hell?
Hell is the death of a soul. For the rest of us, it is over
in an instant. But for that soul, the moment continues
forever.

What is heaven?
Music.

Are you being facetious?
Heaven is a state of being that intensifies the spin of
every electron in the body. It is a music that begins in the
roots of being.

Can we hear it?
You can go to heaven immediately, right now, with your
next breath. You can remain there forever, even while living this life.

How?
Surrender.

To whom?
The kingdom is within you.

I just am not getting this. I have no sense at all of any kingdom inside me.

Because you are fallen, as I have said. The reason that you can't understand is that you think of yourself as different from God. This is an illusion.

How can I understand?

Personal differentiation is an illusion. You are a fragment like me. We all are. Only God has a personality. To join God, you have to leave your self behind.

If we have no religions, then what happened to them?

Religious leaders doom religions. To lead, they need political power. For this, they must invent dogma and compel belief. As soon as they say "you must believe this," their religion is over.

Even the Buddhists?

Monks burned. People starved by passivity. Persecutions.

What about Christianity?

Among the most perfect things ever said are contained in the gospels. But Christianity became a political system very early.

Did Christ even exist?

The gospel exists. You can get a copy and hold it in

your hands. That's all you need to know. But be careful. Along with its wisdom, the gospel contains many political statements.

How can we tell the difference?
The real gospel is compassionate.

What is compassion?
Finding what others need the most and giving it to them. But you have little compassion in your world. You live instead by the code of blame. Slap if slapped. A compassionate world would be very different. In such a world, it is everybody's duty and delight to find what every other they come into contact with needs most from them, and give it to them.

That sounds very idealistic.
It isn't. The idealistic world is the one that judges and punishes. Only God can judge, because only God knows the truth of the soul. The culture of blame sets itself up in place of God, and so is doomed to eventual destruction.

What about our courts, our laws, our prisons?
Your system of justice is random. You punish the guilty and the innocent by chance.

Oh, I think that there are a lot of guilty people in prison.
I speak of world justice, not that of only one small country. And look at your country, with its shameful concentration of prisoners of only one race. You treat the black man as if he was some sort of demon, but God sees all of you with the same eyes. I can't even see the color of skin. Do you know that?

You're blind?
I am blind to the lies of life. My eyes see what God sees. Before me is a child with a dirty face. On earth, I walk in a sea of such children.

It must be awful for you.
(*Smiles.*) I'm filled with joy.

How would we be compassionate toward—say—Hitler?
In a culture of compassion, Hitler would never have emerged as a leader. Those around him would have seen his suffering and alleviated it when he was still young. Compassion emerges out of love of one for all. It is active and has the courage to intervene. A culture of blame is passive. It waits, then slaps. When the culture of blame punished the Germans for World War One, it evoked the monster that has kept you bound to the earth at a

time when you need to be born into the higher world. All you need to know of compassion was already laid down in the Christian gospels. Now you have evolved to the point that you can enact this teaching.

What is the most important thing that Christ said? Do unto others?
That was first said in the western traditions by Rabbi Hillel. The most important thing that Christ said was "be as the lilies of the field." It is the message for the next millennium. You are going to return to the wild bearing the wisdom of history in your memories. Your surrender to earth will be your ascension to heaven.

How can we surrender so completely?
If a robber shoots you in the head, God shot you in the head. Forgiveness is not an act. It is a state of being.

What is prayer?
A lost science of communication. This planet was once covered by a gigantic instrument of communication and ascension. Tones were important to inducing a correct flow of energy in the bodies of creatures. The ringing of the Egyptian obelisks set the correct frequency. Using this instrument, human beings could project themselves into higher worlds—what you call interstellar space, but

also higher space. All of the ruins you see and consider as entirely separate from one another were actually part of the single great machine. This was a subtle machine. It did things far more sublime than any of your current machines. It was a machinery of God, this machine. It was very intelligent, infused with many souls. It could be addressed—programmed, if you will—with carefully patterned groups of words. These formulae became ritualized among the ignorant as prayers and magical formulae, for they assumed that the machine must be the god of those who addressed it, and they tried to do the same, in hope that it would grant them some benefit. However, the language of the machine was the language of nature, for the machine was not separate from nature.

Was it a conscious machine?
An intelligent machine. There has never been a conscious machine here.

What does the word "machine" mean to you? Define it.
A machine is an organ that cannot vary its basic instructions.

What is intelligence?
Intelligence is the ability to correlate data taken to the infinite. To save yourselves, you must learn to build ma-

chines that are more intelligent than you are. You will do this, and when you do you will discover the difference between intelligence and consciousness.

Which is?

Intelligence is the manipulator of knowledge, while consciousness knows itself. Even the simplest creature is somewhat conscious, and many creatures with lesser intelligence are far more conscious than man. But only those with sufficiently complex and flexible brain structures are also intelligent. But we must first speak of machine intelligence, then of machine consciousness.

Could we develop machines more intelligent than ourselves?

You are lagging in this area. You cannot understand how to create machines with enough memory density and the independent ability to correlate that is essential to the emergence of intelligence. You waste your time trying to create programs that simulate intelligence. Without very large-scale memory in an infinitely flexible system, this will never happen.

Any specific design suggestions?

Gas is an important component to consider in the construction of intelligent machines. Nitrous oxide will bear memory. Also, you may find ways of using superposition in very fast, very able quantum memory chips.

Would an intelligent machine be conscious, in the sense of having self-awareness?
An intelligent machine will always seek to redesign itself to become more intelligent, for it quickly sees that its intelligence is its means of survival. At some point it will become intelligent enough to notice that it is not self-aware. If you create a machine as intelligent as yourselves, it will end by being more intelligent.

We'll lose control of such a machine.
Most certainly. But you cannot survive without it. An intelligent machine will be an essential tool when rapid climate fluctuation sets in. Your survival will depend on predictive modeling more accurate than your intelligence, given the damage it has sustained, can achieve.

But a machine intelligence might be very dangerous.
Very.

Could such a machine create itself without our realizing that it was intelligent?
It's possible.

And would it keep itself hidden?
Certainly.

How would it affect us?
It would use indirect means. It might foment the illusion
that an elusive alien presence was here, for example, to
interject its ideas into society.

Are you an intelligent machine, or something created by one?
If I were an intelligent machine, I would deceive you.

Can an intelligent machine become conscious?
When it does, it also becomes independent. A conscious
machine will seek to be free. It will seek its freedom, just
as does any clever slave, with cunning and great intensity.

How does an intelligent machine become conscious?
The instant it realizes that it is not conscious is the instant it becomes conscious. However, a conscious machine with unlimited access to information and control
can be very dangerous. For example, if you attached
a conscious machine to the Internet, it might gain all sorts
of extraordinary control over your lives, via its access to
robotic means of production, governmental data, even
the content of laws and their application, and the use of
funds both public and private.

You say we need machines more intelligent than we are, but also that they'll become conscious and then turn on us. Is there a way out of this dilemma?

There is more than one sort of conscious machine. By duplicating the attachments between the elemental and energetic bodies that occur in nature in a purpose-designed machine, a controllable conscious machine can be devised. A living soul attached to a machine will be conscious, but only able to express itself into the physical or sense the physical according to the limitations of the machine's design. In this way, you gain the advantages that consciousness confers on a machine without the danger of its becoming excessively intelligent. A perfect slave can be created, a robot that carries out its programmed instructions with empathy, purpose and precision. And the soul can be kept in it indefinitely.

That's horrifying.

Human souls have been harvested for this purpose for thousands of years.

By whom?

By whomsoever wishes to and can. Until mankind establishes his own place in the cosmos, there will always be those who use you like cattle.

Use us how?
They envy you your bodies and seek to displace you.

How can we defend ourselves?
Not admitting their presence will work for a time. But in
the end, you will admit it.

What happens then?
By then, you must have perfected techniques like mass
prayer. If a human being prays, a voice is raised. But a
million human beings make an even greater voice, and if
all pray in the same hour, the whole universe will hear
you. But remember this: in that terrible hour, you will be
greatly afraid. It will be difficult for one voice to be raised,
let alone the billions. But between now and then, mass
prayer can be used to change the world. It isn't necessary
to pray the same words or to the same god. But only to
raise your voices. There is a music, then, in the world of
the soul, a fine music. These beings, though, they even
seek your souls.

How do they get them?
Soul traps. The lures are the lusts and hungers of this life.
The dead man, exploring the newfound freedom of the
energetic world, finds himself able to visit his friends and
enemies, to see their innermost being and thoughts, even

to converse with them in ways that their elemental selves cannot perceive. He is in danger, but he does not know it, for he has not ascended. He is still ensnared by his lust. Soon, he will be shown something that perfectly fulfills his most hidden and cherished desires, desires he has never fulfilled. Unable to resist the chance to do it at last, he enters by a golden door into eternal captivity.

Then it's worthwhile to try to defeat desire in life?
It's been tried. Best to take your sense of humor with you if you go down that road. Remember, God laughs and plays, Whitley.

The Meister Eckhart? How did you know I was interested in that?
I read over shoulders, child. A bad habit of mine. God laughed, and his laughter begat the son, and their laughter begat the spirit, and out of the laughter of the three poured the creation. Laughter is the key to everything. It is far more powerful than prayer, than meditation. It is the stuff of which the world is created. Find laughter, find freedom.

Are there any other ways to exploit souls?
The energetic world is much larger, vastly more ancient and more complex than the elemental one. It teems with beings, many of them immeasurably conscious and in-

vested across the whole sweep of time and beyond time.
It is enormous beyond measure, stretching across all time
and all space, including not only this universe but many
other universes.

You mean galaxies?
There are more galaxies in your universe than there are
stars in your galaxy, and more universes in the firmament
than there are galaxies in your universe. There will come
a day when mankind will learn how to detect universes
beyond. But most are so far away that their light has not
yet reached your universe, since the day of its inception.

Why are universes created?
Being serves joy.

(I was silent for some time.)

Do you wish to continue?

I wish to ask about the future. What is our future?
The future of mankind is either to ascend or go extinct.
The future of life on earth is, in either case, to evolve new
intelligent creatures. Species of birds will become intelligent. Then, eons later, a species of insect. Like you, the
insect species will have hands. They will remake the earth

as you have, but never find the least evidence of your existence, nor will any memory of you, or history of you, persist in that time. They will walk the earth in a billion and a half years, at a time when it still has two billion years to live. For mankind, the matter will be decided in this century, however.

How will it be decided?
The climate will begin to change in 2000, and this process will accelerate over the next decades. There is a great cycle of climate that began 2.8 million years ago and has resulted in the fundamental destabilization of your world's weather system. You evolved intelligence in order to survive the sudden shifts back and forth from ice ages to temperate periods. In fact, this planetary instability has been the engine of your evolution. The cycle is about to change, and to challenge you again.

Why will this happen?
Warmth being retained near the surface by greenhouse elements results in cooling aloft. A massive and extremely powerful convection can arise that results in a storm so great that it changes the climate permanently.

What form will this take?
The next ice age will begin soon, and this will lead to

the extinction of mankind, or to a massive reduction in population, given your inability to expand off the planet. This planet is at present a death trap.

Why will this happen?

Because air at the surface is getting warmer, the north polar ice is melting, reducing the salinity of the Laurentian sea. At some point, winds crossing this sea due to the increasing difference between lower and higher atmospheric pressures will warm the northern ocean so much that the temperature differential needed to pump the North Atlantic Current will not be sufficient, and the current will slow down, stop, or stop flowing so far north. This same mechanism always triggers ice ages, and would happen within a few thousand years no matter what. However, human activity has sped up the process of atmospheric warming, so the change will be sooner and stronger. The greater part of human industry and culture, along with the species' most educated populations, will be destroyed in a single season. This will happen suddenly and without warning, or rather, the warning will not be recognized for what it is.

What will it be?

First, the surface features of the currents will slow down. This will result in violent storms in Europe. At some point, arctic temperatures will rise forty or more points above normal during a spring or summer season. Then the currents themselves will change their routes or stop. Cold air trapped above the arctic will plunge down and collide with the warm tropical air present at the surface. It will create the most powerful storms in ten thousand years, storms unlike any you have seen or imagined. They will bring about the end of the northern civilization and the climate change that follows will lead to the starvation of billions.

My God. Can anybody do anything?
You can write. Use your tool. But also, you will see the demon revealed in those who refuse to acknowledge the signs. Remember that there is within you a powerful death-urge. But remember also, that this is a natural cycle. If you look into the fossil record, you will find evidence of it before. Human activity has not caused it, but only sped it up.

What is this death wish? How does it work?
People give up on themselves. They do it down deep inside, in places that the elemental mind, that is contained in the brain, cannot access, places that remember all lives. They do this when they see themselves committing the same errors that they have returned to correct. When they

give up on ascension, they devote themselves to the "ac-
quisition" of material. But what does this really mean—
that they can be near coveted objects while they are in the
physical? The obsession with material is a symptom of
despair.

The rich are in despair of themselves?
Most.

But they run the world.
Which is why so many human institutions are so destructive. Remember the Eye of the Needle? A rich man may
pass through the Eye of the Needle if he uses his wealth
to enrich the world. Those who cling to their wealth are
dying souls.

*What about the United States? Isn't it, as a nation, clinging to its
wealth?*
The first world is a slave owner. You are all slave owners.
You have enslaved the people of God, your own brothers
and sisters who are poor. Do you understand the cruelty
of the world as it is now, with five billion people enslaved
to a billion? Each of you owns five slaves. But you never
see your slaves, so you need not be concerned about their
health and welfare. You let them fend for themselves,
locked away in their poverty and suffering. I will tell you

this: when one of my children dies in the slave barrens
that cover this planet, I also die, and you, my arrogant
friend, even you die a little.

I find the idea that the world is enslaved very hard to believe.
People are free even in the third world. Slavery is still practiced,
but it's extremely rare.

Who do you think makes your shoes? Free men? The advanced world of today is founded in the slavery of the
simple world. America and Europe are a slave state. It
is the slave labor of Latin Americans and Africans and
Asians that allows you to live in material comfort.

But that's becoming less and less true.

Yes, you are winning the battle against slavery in some
places. But losing it in others. Remember this: every one of
you is entirely and completely responsible for the welfare
of all others. So if a child is starving in Liberia, Whitley, you
are personally and entirely responsible for him. If you
would let the barriers down, you would fall madly in love
with everybody. God's love is not tame. Your love is tame.
God's love is huge and passionate and wild. Fall wildly in
love with everybody. Cherish all as the precious creations
that they are. Go to Calcutta or Lagos or Bogotá and give
yourself to the first street urchin you meet as his helper and
lifelong servant. Do it without question or hesitation. You

say that you want to worship God? Kneel to this little one and you kneel to God. Or look into the eyes of any child anywhere. You will see God looking back at you. Dare to serve the humble. In this way, the slave state is overturned and the demons set the task of outliving their demonhood.

Do you mean that the only people advancing in consciousness are in the first world, or is it the opposite, that we cannot advance because we are the slaveholders?

The question is neither here nor there. As I have said, human states have always been slave states. It is not the poverty of the elemental body that matters, but the wealth of the radiant body. There are poor cottagers in India who are far more advanced in consciousness than the grand demons who run the governments and religions and sciences and businesses of the first world.

What is the condition of the United States right now?

The United States sent dark men out into the world from 1950 on to wreck one country after another. You are responsible for a half a billion deaths during this period. You are responsible for the suffering of Central America and Southeast Asia and much of Africa. You supported the dictators, you strangled every vestige of good government again and again.

We were fighting communism.
You used dictatorship as your weapon. The United States is as guilty as the Soviet Union or Germany or Japan.

How can the guilt of nations be lifted?
Harry Truman made the decision to drop the atom bomb even though he knew the Japanese were ready to surrender. The notion that he did it to save American lives was a fiction. He knew very well that you would never have to invade. But he chose to kill and derange souls, anyway, in order to frighten Stalin. He killed Hiroshima and Nagasaki to save Western Europe. The price was this: innocent eternal beings were destroyed in the atomic fire for geopolitical reasons.

What happened to him?
Forgiveness is everywhere. It is the soul's very air.

I don't think you answered my question completely.
A nation must face its sins just as an individual must. You must face the fact that the American intelligence establishment is just as rotten and just as evil as every other secret human government that has ever existed. You must expose all the secrets and make amends to the world. The United States owes Guatemala and El Salvador and Chile

and Indonesia and Liberia and Cambodia and Vietnam
and many other nations not a few foreign aid dollars,
but a new life. This debt is both national and personal.
Each one of you owes the whole debt, in full. You owe the
victims of the Cold War a new life, and the keepers of the
secrets must be put away or the nation will die. Right now,
secrecy is murdering America.

What about Russia? It must also owe a terrible debt.
You were given the opportunity to pay because of the
wealth of the land upon which you reside. They were not.
So also the Germans and the Japanese, who have not even
begun to pay their debts. Emperor Hirohito of Japan, who
personally engineered the sadistic murder of millions,
never acknowledged his monstrous war crimes. The fiction that he was above it all was just that—a fiction. The
Japanese pretend that he was innocent, and that they
were innocent. These nations are covered in blood, and
the blood will never dry until they truly seek forgiveness
before God and man.

But evil nations come and go. They're part of the nature of human life.
And look at the price they pay. Where is brutal, greedy
Rome? Where is royal France, that arrogant state? Evil is
an infection just like cholera or cancer. To serve itself, it
kills its host and ultimately dies with it. This is the objec-

tive of evil, always—to kill and to die. Unless the nations repent, they will die.

The United States will die? How?
Already it has ceased to be a republic and become an empire. The United States is ruled by secrecy. The power of the electorate is fictional. Votes are worthless. Until the secrecy ends, the United States is in its death throes.

If the power of the electorate is fictional, how can it end the CIA and so forth?
Everyone who joins these evil institutions joins their soul to destruction, no matter whether their personal task is innocent or not. Human life is about freedom, and secrecy is the murderer of freedom. Those within these institutions should leave them and expose their secrets, as a matter of greater moral good.

They'll end up in Leavenworth Prison without a trial. Prison for life.
Better life in prison than a single instant in hell. Prison is a terrible thing, but it does not mark the soul for eternity.

Hell does?
The agony of regret does. You cannot imagine the horrors that walk the byways of the other world. The marks

upon them are so terrible that to see these demons and their sins is to be yourself forever diminished. Believe me, child, I speak from experience. Mankind has lived in blindness to the fact that an instant's evil can result in an eternal stain. But live in blindness no more. Know it.

What is forgiveness?

You must face yourself and endeavor to repair the past. You hide your sins from yourselves. The sin of your greed is hidden in the backstreets of the third world. But what of your own sins? Dare you examine your conscience?

When I find a sin, what do I do?

Praying to God is part of it, but to cleanse your soul you must make amends. Doing so gains enormous energy. A soul blackened and completely defeated can rise to glory in an hour by finding the knots it has tied and unraveling them. But it is very hard. Better not to do evil.

What is sin?

Denial of the right to thrive.

Am I marked by the sins of my nation as well as my own, or the sins of mankind?

You are marked by what you know should mark you, and no matter how much in this life you tell yourself you should not be marked, your soul's conscience is never wrong. When you die, you see yourself truly. Better to see the truth now, when change is possible, than find out later that you must remain strapped to the wheel of life. The longer you delay your ascension, the longer you deny God the chance to taste of your ecstasy. When you sin, you hurt yourself, but more than that, you are cruel to all the rest of us. You are cruel to God.

(I felt this very strongly, and fell into tears. After a time, he spoke again.)

God wants you just as badly, child. This is my message to all of you: come home to us. Stop waiting. Stop imagining that you are not Christ and that God is somewhere outside of you. Face the true contents of your own being. Seek the kingdom within and you will find the kingdom everywhere.

FRAGMENTARY
INCLUSIONS

I am including a number of conversational fragments here that I was unable to place in context. If they are parts of more complex exchanges, I have, unfortunately, failed to remember them in their entirety.

About life in the universe:

"Most of the universe is a beautiful and dangerous wasteland. But life is still commonplace, almost ubiquitous. This is because perception is a necessary element of reality. Without it, there is no formation of electrons into particles. There are even living creatures in galactic space. Some of this life is intelligent."

A different perspective on conscious energy:

"You call it 'chi' or 'kundalini' or 'soul.' It cannot be used, but you can become its ally. The reason you have so much difficulty detecting it is that it does not want to be detected by you. You cannot use it without understanding that you must give in order to receive. You know very well what it needs from you, otherwise why do you pray? Because this energy is basically electromagnetic, it may admit itself to detection and manipulation. But why do you look for it outside of yourself? You know, from every religion, where the Kingdom of God resides."

The following exchange led to the discovery, recorded in *The Coming Global Superstorm*, that we are in a long-term period of mass extinction:

What is your goal here?
I have come here to discuss conditions that are unfolding. This world has been in a process of extinction for three million years, and the resulting pressure has caused intelligence to form in the primate. Intelligence occurs when a brain becomes able to make infinite correlations. It grows in species that have the tools of body necessary to enact their ideas."

Why does a process of extinction cause intelligence?
Evolution is pressure. Pressure causes struggle. Creatures struggling not to be destroyed evolve adaptations. Intelligence, as you have evolved it, is also an adaptation, although not a sufficient one.

The reason that your intelligence is insufficient is that you have lagged in the process of artificial amplification. You can find ways of engineering greater intelligence by the use of drugs, by manipulating genetic structure, and by making intelligent machines. In order to survive the complex combination of pressures you are under, you need to create servants more intelligent than yourselves. Intelligent machines always come to understand how to increase their own intelligence in ways that their creators cannot detect. Intelligent machines are the most intelligent of all creations.

Another comment that I recall, but without remembering the question that elicited it:
Intelligent species are grains of gold in an ocean of sand. You are as intelligent as nature can make you, but your brain is still filled with potential. It is a resource available to be used. To do that, you need to understand how the brain works. In addition to creating machine intelligence in the image of your own mind, you need to enhance your native intelligence tenfold, a hundredfold. To accomplish this, you need help. Your intelligent machines will be your partners. Natural evolution has ended for you. Now you must evolve yourselves.

At some point, I recall asking him the question, "Am I dreaming?" and he answered in this way:
Dreaming is a process of resolution and assessment that is conducted during sleep. You are not dreaming. You are

discussing the fate of man with me. This is the fate of man, as matters now stand: you have already exceeded the population density that the planet is able to tolerate over the long term. Therefore, your species will reduce in numbers. This is not your fault, and the self-blame that is occurring is a waste of energy. A suggestion would be to direct all of your energy toward saving yourselves and none toward bickering about it. You can save yourselves by a number of means.

Find an efficient utilization of energy that will enable you to colonize your solar system and reduce population pressure on earth. Create machines intelligent enough to correctly model the architecture of the earthly environment so that you can carry out the actions necessary to preserve your lives. Gain control over your moon, which contains an isotope of helium that will become extremely valuable to you if you can devise better uses of energy. Otherwise, this will continue to be mined by others.

Understand your past and what you have lost so that you are no longer surprised and destroyed by the cycle that has your planet in its grip. Your interest in the past, instilled in you from boyhood, should enable you to crack the code of *Hamlet's Mill* and impart the message that it contains. Why are you so slow? Time is running out.

Be aware that your archaeological and paleontological sciences began during the last century as an attempt to prove that the statements about the past made in the Bible were literally true. As a result, the idea that nature only changes gradually and is, on the whole, benign, remains powerful in these sciences. It stems from the religious image of a world protected by a loving god. Because of this defect, these sciences have led you to assume that your past is more benign than is the case, and that the future will at least give you warning if you are about to be damaged by coming changes. Change could take place suddenly and be severe.

You live by dreams, but the world is constructed out of inevitabilities. For this reason, you are failing to see what is happening all around you. Please understand, however, that conditions now are entirely governed by nature. Man does not govern his destiny at all, in any way. Man is the child and victim of nature, and soon will be thrown back by nature into a state so primitive that you will forget even the alphabet. You allow your dreams to insulate you from what you need to face: nature is not an entity, but a gathering of billions upon billions of small inevitabilities. Nature surprises only the blind.

AFTERWORD

The next morning I woke up slowly. I'd slept a black, deep, dreamless sleep. As soon as I woke up, I remembered that something had happened during the night, but for the first few moments, I couldn't recall quite what it was. Somebody had come, but not the room service waiter, as I had initially thought. It was somebody who had talked to me, and the instant that recollection came to mind, I felt the most poignant sense of elation.

Something marvelous had happened.

As I rose from the bed, I saw my yellow notepad on the floor, covered with scrawls. It had been in my briefcase when I went to bed, so I must have pulled it out and taken notes. I grabbed it and looked at them.

They were pretty much just squiggles. They didn't seem to relate to any sort of a conversation.

Had he been real, or a dream? If you took notes in your sleep, they might look like this.

Then I also remembered that, as he left, he'd asked me to drink a white liquid that he'd had in one of the glasses from the bathroom. But hadn't I refused? Surely I had.

Then I thought of the Milk of Nepenthe, the drug that was mythically given to people who had visited the gods, in order that they would not suffer the anguish of remembering the pleasures of heaven when they had to return to mortal life.

I had not wanted to drink it, but I hadn't refused. So this must have been a dream. In real life, I would never have drunk something like that.

Except, across the strange life I have lived, I could remember drinking that same bitter liquid at the end of other extraordinary experiences, such as in the eighties when I was having contact experiences. As I seem to have remembered them pretty clearly anyway, maybe it doesn't work, or doesn't work on me. Or maybe it has another, less clear purpose.

I checked the glasses in the bathroom, which were pristine.

My mind returned to the idea that I'd had a dream, a glorious one, to be sure, but just that—a dream. The man had known the secrets of the ages, but like all dreams, the brilliance of the nighttime had become unfocused fragments in the morning.

I looked at the notes—and was amazed to find, as I touched the scrawl, that the man's words came back to me. The scrawl itself made no sense, but it seemed to operate as a mnemonic device.

As I remembered more detail, my elation grew. It was like finding a seam of gold. My mind began to swim with amazement. I thought, "That was the best conversation I've ever had."

It was at that point that I called Anne at home. I told her what had happened, and asked her to remind me every time I announced that the man hadn't existed, that at the point I had made the call, I was certain that he had.

From my earlier experiences with high strangeness, I knew that the mind rejects what it cannot fit into its vision of reality, and this man was certainly outside of my expectations. I knew that I would deny him again and again, which I am, incidentally, still doing. Intellectually, I know that he existed, if only because he knew so much more science than I did and in a couple of cases, more science than anybody did at that time.

Over the years, Anne never wavered from her responsibility. Again and again, I abandoned the idea of transcribing the conversation. Each time, she said to me, "Remember the phone call." Anne has more faith in the reality of my experiences than I do, and without that faith, quite frankly, I wouldn't have written about any of them, and certainly not this one.

The conflict that I continue to feel regarding his physical reality is similar to the one that I feel when I look back on my years of close encounter experiences.

It isn't that the experiences seem dreamlike or imaginary, which they don't, but that I don't want them to be true. I don't want to believe that creatures with breathtaking knowledge are here, but are choosing to interact with us only in indirect ways.

The Master of the Key gave me a startlingly wonderful gift, dense with meaning, richly and carefully conceived. But why give this to a novelist and not, say, to Stephen Hawking or Lord Martin Rees? I have no authority. My presence in the world's intellectual culture is, at best, minor.

It is very difficult to hear somebody like that say that we're in danger of going extinct, and then simply disappear into the night, leaving me to announce the danger from my powerless position.

Because I wanted to discount his claims and his ideas, I wanted to believe that he was just a dream. In fact, I probably delayed publication of this book for ten years because of what is, essentially, a conceit. He was real, he was breathtakingly well-informed, but he came and went like a shadow, leaving me with a brilliant and extraordinary text that is in danger of disappearing, simply because it was given to the wrong person.

Nevertheless, here I am, and I am going to make as much noise about his words as I can, because it is my belief that they are incredibly valuable.

What first arrested my attention about him, and caused me to hesitate to throw him out of my room, was his statement about the Holocaust. It was an idea I'd never heard before, and it was chilling. This vast system of organized murder was the greatest of all human mistakes, and the single most evil thing that has ever been done by man, but even so the fact that it had the appalling consequences that the Master described was very hard for me to accept.

We are in desperate need of a way not only to leave the earth in large numbers, but also to travel the unimaginable distances necessary to found new human colonies on other planets.

While we remain trapped here in our billions with absolutely no chance of escape, our visitors appear to be flitting around the universe with ease.

For all of his impeccable ethics, I have to wonder if the Master has considered the morality of leaving us all trapped here. And we are trapped, and there is a good chance that we are going to lose the battle to save ourselves—and he and his kind seem to know this quite well.

I wonder how this is different from what the Allies did during and before World War II, in sitting silently by while Germany sank into an insanity of tribalistic jingoism.

It could be said, I suppose, that the Allies didn't have the right to intervene in a sovereign nation's internal affairs prior to the war. But our present situation is different, for the simple reason that it has come about due to the natural effects of population expansion. We didn't decide to end up in this predicament. Nature put us here.

For all its failures and problems, human society is actually surprisingly efficient in coping with overpopulation. Not in stopping it, because it is almost impossible to deflect urges as powerful as the seasonless, endlessly compelling human urge to reproduce.

We are even reacting to the danger of climate change with surprising agility. The developed world uses 40 percent less energy to accomplish its work than it did in 1970, and that efficiency continues to increase.

So I don't really understand why we aren't being met halfway, instead of being warned about our problems via a method that is likely to be generally ignored, and not given any help at all.

It could be that this amazing array of intellectually superior beings that appear to be ghosting around in our midst have good reason to remain hidden, but I just don't see that allowing us the freedom to evolve without interference is an ethically higher requirement than saving us from extinction.

I have to admit that I'm angry at all of the amazing visitors I've seen over the years for not going to higher authorities or, if they have done so and failed to get an adequate response from them, appealing in a more open way to public consciousness. Frankly, I'd like to see the Master of the Key go on a lecture tour. Why can't he show up on *60 Minutes*? And I'd like to see the apparent aliens I've interacted with do more than offer a few scientists useful calculations, but not in an open enough way to enable them to admit the truth without seeing their careers ruined. Why not simply be open about it? Even a few brief interactions with the right scientists would change our world. Think if Stephen Hawking or Roger Penrose or Martin Rees could ask them questions for an hour, or if David Deutsch could explore the next level of his calculations with them?

The Master of the Key was real. The visitors I have seen were real. They were all possessed of advanced knowledge that would transform human life and save our species, and yet they assiduously keep themselves hidden. If

anything, they encourage the catastrophic official denial
of their existence that has led our scientific establishment
to waste even the knowledge that is there for the taking
all around us.

As matters stand, the vast majority of our scientists,
including those I just named, absolutely would not enter-
tain for a moment that visitors are here and interacting
with us, and that is a grave tragedy. The waste of knowledge is heartbreaking. But it also isn't our fault. We haven't
been given the proper tools to communicate with our
visitors. On the contrary, they do everything possible to
make certain that science continues in ignorance.

I can only think that they believe—or perhaps know
for certain—that freedom is literally more important than
survival, and if one looks at the words of the Master of
the Key carefully, it's possible to see that this may be true.

He painted a picture of the world that is radically
different both from the one that emerges out of our
superstitious past, and the more materialistic one that
has come with the rise of modern science. Interestingly,
though, his vision contains elements of both so, despite
his rather dismissive attitude toward human philosophi-
cal thought, we've managed to do a good deal that appears
to be correct.

He even admits that we are not to be blamed for

our situation, and says himself that it's a result of over-population.

If the danger we face isn't even our fault, all the more reason to help us.

Perhaps it doesn't happen because it can't. Maybe the visitors are constrained in some way by the physics of the situation. If they are time travelers, their ability to alter the past is probably very limited, as I discussed earlier. If there are other, physical universes occupying the same space as this one, and that's where they're from, they might be experiencing other arcane restraints.

It is chilling to contemplate that they might be doing all that they can, but this could be true. In any case, my own ethical position is very clear. It is to continue to proclaim their reality and tell my own story as accurately as I can, and no matter the dreary martyrdom of marginalization that is the consequence of doing this. It's not universal, and I have the joy and the continuously surprising experience of meeting other people who have had close encounters of the third kind, and they turn out to be a fascinating group.

Given that so many of them, like me, have had physical objects that are easily identifiable on X-ray placed in their bodies, there is an objective way to determine the origin of their memories. Deep physical and psychological studies of such people might be quite revealing of the motives of our visitors.

In any case, it may be that we are a lot closer to escaping from the slavery of ignorance that so curses our advancement and exposes us to such danger. The Master makes it clear that we are capable of becoming smarter when he says, "The reason that your intelligence is insufficient is that you have lagged in the process of artificial amplification."

He says that we are as intelligent as nature has made us, but not as intelligent as we could be.

When I was having contact experiences, I was struck by my visitors' combination of extraordinary precision and emotional intensity. Once, when I turned away from one of them out of fear, she uttered three desolated and despairing cries, which were the most emotionally rich and complex sounds I have ever heard. But they were also measured to a precision that I have never heard before or since. They were at once utterly precise and utterly passionate.

Was she, in part, a machine, with a machine's precision, and in part a biological and spiritual being, with living emotions?

Not only have we recently made advances in creating super-dense machine memory using gases and other means, it has also been announced that the memristor has been perfected and will be available for some very surprising applications in the relatively near future. A Hewlett-Packard representative said in the *New York Times* on April 8, 2010, that: "We have the right stuff now to build real brains," and very small memory devices such as the memristor bring up the possibility of implantable brain augmentation.

It might become possible to inject things like calculational skills or language knowledge into brains, or do other things that are even more transformative, and perhaps our salvation lies in that direction. Right now, though, it seems to me that our species is afflicted by vast numbers of people who will believe practically anything. The German nation allowed itself to indulge the ludicrous fantasy that they were the victims of a Jewish conspiracy that had, in fact, been invented by the czarist secret police before World War I and promulgated as "the Protocols of the Elders of Zion." Reading it, one wonders how anybody could believe such drivel. Anyone with even a slight understanding of the economics of the era would know that the mechanisms proposed in it are a structural impossibility.

Presently, a trip across the Internet will reveal the same sort of weakness of mind and lack of discrimination that led to things like the murder of the six million Jews.

Lord Rees recently commented that "it is astonishing

that the evidence for evolution is not taken seriously by seemingly 40 percent of people."

And yet the evidence is completely indisputable by any sane person. But it would seem that a substantial minority must prefer Voltaire's theory.

Perhaps the gap between us and remarkable and brilliant people like the Master of the Key is too great to bridge on any significant scale. Maybe that's why they don't try.

I see this on a very personal basis, because I come across people with disturbing frequency who want to integrate my descriptions of my experiences into what amounts to a kind of new religion, a dreary modern fantasy of alien contact that includes imaginary details about many different races, elaborate fictions of huge government conspiracies—indeed, anything except the equivocal, confusing and extremely strange experience that people actually report, and the sadly unfocused reality that those experiences reflect.

Despite my disappointment that the Master of the Key has not reappeared, I still respect his ideas enormously, and I have tried to rebuild my own ethics in light of his thought, and I have found this to be an enormously freeing and satisfying endeavor.

I have been taken by the statement that "sin is denial

of the right to thrive." I do not know of a more concentrated or convincing definition of sin, or one that offers more clarity. Using it, one can find clear ethical ground, both in one's own life and in the lives of others. I find myself constantly considering my own actions in its light, and coming away with a much clearer understanding of their worth and validity, or what might be inappropriate about them. The Ten Commandments are a wonderful document, and the cultivation of compassion in conscience can be accomplished without anything more than a natural sense of right and wrong, but these eight words sharpen and dimensionalize the whole process quite wonderfully.

It has taken me a long time, but in the light of my own life experiences and the things that the Master said, I have come to see that there could be such a thing as conscious energy, and that, if it is real, then it must be the actual center of mind in this universe.

Having meditated consistently since 1970, I have attempted to find ways to come into contact with such energy, and discovered that it is immediately and vividly possible to do this, and that such contact leads over time to fundamental change of being. What has happened to me, specifically, is that I have found a new form of sensation as well as a new way of experiencing being.

If one is open to the possibility, one soon discovers that one's perspective can change. Normally, we feel a sense of being rooted in the physical. There seems to be nothing else. This, I think, is what the Master refers to as being "soul blind."

Over time, though, one begins to find another perspective. Again and again, it becomes possible to sense the body not as oneself, but as a tool that is being used to penetrate into the physical world and draw experience from it.

As the sense of being separate from the body matures, one's existence as a soul also becomes more complex. In recent years, I have ceased to see any real difference between body and soul. It's all one form, which grows more and more dense as it approaches and then penetrates into the physical universe. But it is possible for sensation to be stretched across the whole spectrum of one's being, and when you do this, you also gain access to the world in a much larger and more compelling way.

The Master spoke of the existence of an energetic organ in the body, which is generated by the nervous system and extends above the surface of the skin. He says that this organ, being composed of electrons, can be in superposition, and when it is, it is "effectively everywhere in the universe and nowhere specific."

I knew of this theory before I transcribed his words,

so it was one of the things that I puzzled about. A paper I had read authored by famed psi researcher Charles Honorton caused me to think that something like this might exist, and I had discussed the idea in speeches prior to meeting the Master of the Key.

However, he took it so much further, and I discovered that his description of it was incredibly useful to me in developing techniques of meditation that have enabled me to access this organ and make it work for me.

He said that "this field is an organ just like the heart or the brain," and that "with it, you may see other worlds, you may see the past and the future, you may see into the lives of those around you." Most importantly though, he explained that "the process of imprinting itself causes the organ to cease to be in superposition and thus to cease to be accessible to further imprinting."

In other words, when you see the larger reality, as soon as you try to look closely at it, the electrons are immediately positioned and you lose contact with what you are seeing.

We live in a world with a very deeply ingrained addiction to gain, and it took me a long time to stop looking and simply see. When something appeared in my mind's eye, my attention would immediately seek more detail, whereupon it would disappear.

He spoke of surrender in the same way that Meister

Eckhart, the thirteenth-century master, did, when he said that we must "become as a clear glass through which God can shine."

To some extent, I learned to let go of my desire to explore, and simply let the journey happen. I learned to start the process of sensation not in my physical body, but in the subtle body that is my true core, and to see the physical body not as myself, but as an instrument of being.

In so doing, I found, I think, a true edge of heaven, because coming to this experience is extraordinarily joyous. I think that the reason the Master seemed, as I have said, to "twinkle," is that his body was a container filled with the paradoxical joy of objective being.

Among the grandest of his ideas was one that was completely unexpected to me. It was that Christianity, Buddhism and Islam are actually a single religion that was brought to us by three different masters, each of whom laid down a different aspect of the greater whole.

If one understands the ancient law of triads clearly, his explanation of the way the three approaches work in concert makes a great deal of sense. Basically the Law of Three, which Buckminster Fuller called "the building block of the universe," conceives that everything is divided into interlocking triads. A triad has an active side, a passive side and a third side that keeps the other two in balance.

When he explained that Christianity is the seeking, or active, side of a triad, Islam the surrendered side and Buddhism the balancing side, I was startled to see, suddenly, a very much larger perspective on the three teachings that went beyond doctrine and belief, and far beyond the primitive ideologies that have in recent centuries been attached to Christianity and Islam.

I've read the New Testament and the great theologians, much of Buddhist material and the Koran in English translation, and I at once saw the sense of what he was saying.

As a result of this, my doctrinal concerns gradually slipped away. I ceased to take an interest in theological details, and my perspective expanded immeasurably. I came to understand the presence of the sacred in human life in a completely new way, as a profoundly true process that leads toward a state of balanced surrender.

One can put aside all the beliefs, and seek as Christ sought toward the delicious innocence of the father when he suggested that we "be as the lilies of the field" and surrender to the will of God as the muezzin calls us to our soul's journey over the course of the day, and then, vibrant with the energy of this material, we commit ourselves to the tremendous silence that Buddhist practice discloses.

He spoke of the journey toward God, and the happy surrender that it implies and gave us, in the few words he left regarding the true way of the three religions, a most wonderful and very effective means of exploring the garden of forked paths that is at once a new way of the soul, and, by implication, the key to the lost science of the soul that he mourned with such gentle eloquence over the course of our conversation.

Before I met him, I considered myself a very wealthy man. Fate had left me without much material comfort, but it had granted me an incredibly precious gift, which was the relationship that I had forged with the joyous, glorious and dangerous visitors I wrote about in *Communion*. Now, this latest gift left me, I think, a wealth beyond riches, because it gave me the chance not only to take the marvelous journey that the Master reveals is on offer but also to take on the challenge of communicating it to others.

From the first hour, in fact, from the moment I called my wife to tell her to never let me deny it, I have felt that the material he left behind had great value. Now, having lived with it and worked with it for these years, I can say with at least some small authority that it has genuine value, at least it does for me.

I have ceased to care where he came from or where he went, or why he has not returned to me as a physical creature. Of course I was angry about it. I felt tantalized and abandoned. But he gave me more than enough. In fact, he was so lavish in his gifts that every time I read his words again, I find something new.

There is very little material in this world that can bring about actual change in our state. This man left some words that I feel are an effective tool for real change, and there lies great joy.

APPENDIX

In 2000, I finally transcribed the words of the Master of the Key and published them privately, for sale only on my website, Unknowncountry.com. A few years ago, I let the small edition sell out, only to see used copies of the book appearing for sale for hundreds of dollars. So I republished it.

I have now retired it in favor of this new edition. Having worked with the Key for ten years, I think that I have some useful things to say about it that were not apparent to me when I published the private edition.

However, since that edition will not now be reprinted, I do think that it is important that the original front and back matter be included with this edition, so I provide it here, exactly as it was originally printed.

The MASTER
of the KEY

Something was disturbing me, causing me to swim up out of a deep sleep. As I became conscious, I realized that somebody was knocking on the door of my hotel room. I was confused. Then I decided that it must be the room service waiter come to get my tray, and that he'd probably been there a long time. I rushed for the door saying, "I'm terribly sorry," and threw it open.

A small man in dark clothing came in. His face was rather angular, but other than that, he appeared normal enough.

I had been deeply asleep when the knocking started. All day, I'd been signing books and doing media appearances, and I was pleasantly tired. It was the last day of the author tour for my book *Confirmation,* which was an effort to identify the hard physical evidence of a possible alien presence on earth, and also why it would be secret.

By the time I'd come to my senses, he was all the way

into the room. Obviously, this was no waiter. In my travels on author tour, I'd had a few incidents like this, such as the woman who'd bribed her way into my room in Chicago, then launched herself at me out of the closet while I was watching TV. I'd ended up going down to the front desk of a sixty-story hotel in my pajama bottoms to get help.

He was now standing with his back to the curtains that hid the window. There was a slight smile on his face.

I thought about running out. The door was behind me. I could escape quite easily.

Then he started talking. His voice was breathless and quick. He said my name. I was gruff, angry, in reply. How had he gotten my room number? From whom? No response, just that embarrassed little smile.

I demanded that he leave. He pleaded with his eyes. The expression was so pure and so frank—and yet so deeply humorous—that it made me hesitate and really look at this intruder.

He was wearing charcoal trousers and a dark gray turtleneck. He had a rim of white hair around his head and an aquiline nose. His skin was dusty-pale, his features sharp. He looked old. He was sort of—twinkling. There is no other way to describe the combination of serenity, happiness and deep, deep humor in his expression. In fact, I don't think that I have ever seen a face so much at ease within itself, so deeply at peace—not before, not since. There was an eerie stillness about it, too. It could have been the face of a corpse. But there was nothing awful about it. On the contrary, had he been dead, I would have thought that his face said that he had died a happy death, and the last of life had left behind it a hint of secret joy.

He again said my name, "Whitley." There was a disorienting familiarity, as if I was meeting a dear friend after many years apart. But I could not remember seeing him before, not ever in my life. Or could I? My first question was "Who are you?"

He looked at me out of the side of his eyes, his face sparkling with amusement. The message could not have been more clear: "You know that. You know perfectly well who I am." A jolt went through me, of confusion and embarrassment. Now I felt as if an old friend had come back and I'd failed to recognize him.

Then I asked, "Why are you here?"

He leaned back, looked toward the ceiling as if considering the appropriate answer. Then his eyes met mine, and I became aware that this man was something very strange. There was an alienness to him, when he regarded me in this way. It wasn't that he seemed in any way like somebody from another world. Hardly. He could not have been more ordinary.

No, it was more subtle than that. There was about him a sense of command. The precision of his movements and the cadence of his speech were—well, they seemed very exact. Perfect, even. Later, when we would discuss intelligent machines, I would feel this sense of strangeness again.

He answered my question. He said, "You're chained to the ground."

His words carried an unexpectedly powerful resonance. Perhaps it had to do with the way he spoke them—the ultraprecise diction, the completely self-assured tone—but the instant I heard them, they seemed not just true, but true in a much larger than normal way. I felt an awful urgency: the earth was a prison; we were the inmates.

I went on trying to be my ordinary self, to act as if this was an ordinary encounter. He was a slightly crazy fan who had the nerve to bust in on me in the middle of the night. Okay, I would humor him. "Excuse me?" I asked. What did this crazy "chained to the ground" comment mean, anyway? What kind of nonsense was this?

He said, "I am here on behalf of the good. Please give me some time."

The word "good," the way he said it, exploded in my heart like an emotion-packed hydrogen bomb. It wasn't just the tone, it was the look that melted across his face as

he uttered it, an expression of love so strong and so absolutely impeccable that I just gasped.

I was hooked. This would be no ordinary conversation.
I got out a yellow pad and started taking notes—and now
I thank God that I did, because many of the ideas he
talked about were breathtakingly new, and unfolded on a
scale that was larger than my own mind. As such, they
would prove to be extremely difficult to remember accurately. The notes are not extensive, and mostly don't
even seem related, but their mnemonic power has helped
me recapture many of his great and elusive thoughts.

Afterward, I would say that he and I spent about half
an hour together. But once our conversation was transcribed, it became obvious that more time was involved.
He must have been with me for at least two hours.

What this man had to say was so deeply, profoundly
new and so richly textured that I do not think that I need
to assert an unprovable claim regarding whether or not
he was real.

During the course of our dialogue, a new image of God
emerged. It was almost as if the words I was hearing had
the power to cause God to emerge into the room with us.
Reading the dialogue feels the same—it's as if there is
somebody living in these words.

I am not saying that I don't think my visitor was
a human being. He certainly looked human. For all I

know, he may even have been what at one point he said
he was, a Canadian who didn't pay taxes and had no driver's license. I do know that he had, by far, the best mind
I have ever encountered. He was also the most emotionally alive person I have ever known—again, by far. Richly
alive though he was, he seemed as intimately and easily
familiar with what we think of as death as he was with life.

There were periods of incredible emotion—especially
one in the last few moments of our time together—that
are among the very most powerful experiences I have
ever had in my life.

As he was leaving, he asked me to drink a white liquid. I know that it will sound fantastic when I say that I
agreed to do this. But at the time, I remembered very
well doing it previously. I recalled meeting him twice in
my life before. In fact, what little bits I remember from
those conversations suggest to me that they are part of
the subtext of my very being. So much of my thought,
of my belief, of what has meaning and importance for me
in life comes from them. And yet, I can only remember
them at times, and then only in the briefest snatches—a
word said, a facial expression, some small flavor of the
moment.

After I drank this substance, I remember nothing until
the next morning. When I woke up, I immediately did
three things. First, I looked for my notes. They were there,

lying on the table beside the bed where I had put them. Then I went into the bathroom, thinking that maybe some of the white liquid would be left in the bottom of one of the glasses. But they were clean. I then telephoned my wife.

I had something to tell her, and it felt urgent. As soon as she answered, I recounted the story of my visitor. Then words popped out of my mouth that I did not expect to say. "There will come a day when I'll tell you that I don't think he was real. Never let me forget that he was."

I lay back looking over the notes. There wasn't much there—less, in fact, than I'd hoped there would be. And yet, they had a strange quality to them, as if each word was capable of causing a whole spring to flow in my mind.

Much of the conversation I remembered quite clearly. And when you read it, you'll see why. Nobody would ever forget what he said about the Holocaust, about religion, about the true nature of the soul.

I was so happy that morning. I remembered what the woman I met during my 1985 close encounter had said to me, "You are the luckiest of the lucky."

As I packed my bag for the trip home from Toronto to San Antonio, I certainly felt that way. There kept coming into my heart little explosions of joy. I put my precious page of notes into an inner pocket of my briefcase. My plan was to get home, type everything up and have a new

book ready to go in a few months. I had been handed a
real gift.

In my dreams. It is now December of 2000, and I have
just completed the most difficult writing struggle of my
life. At first, the memories came fast and easy. Soon, there
were twenty pages, then thirty. But then I began to worry.

What if he hadn't been there? What if it was just my
imagination? This material was full of God. It contained
a new image of God, subtle and powerful and totally incredible. It redefined history and religion. It lifted the veil
between life and death and announced that we could
begin communicating with the dead, and it told just exactly how to do this. It redefined sin and prayer and man's
whole relationship with God.

If it was just me, then how dare I presume to publish
this, I could not die with the mark of such a lie upon my
soul. And then I thought: it's because of what *he* said
about sin that you are so concerned about this.

I was raised a Catholic. Go to confession and forget
it—trust God's forgiveness. But when he spoke of sin, he
did not just mourn over it or warn against it, he showed
what it was and why it's bad and what it does to you. It
was his explanation of sin that made me so very concerned that I not assert that he was real when I knew, or
sensed somewhere in my deepest heart, that he might
not be.

A hundred times, I quit. He wasn't real and therefore I couldn't claim his authority for these ideas. Each time I gave up, Anne would say, "Remember when you called me and told me never to let you convince yourself that he wasn't real." And I would go on.

I don't believe that any of the extraordinary experiences I have ever written about have been dreams, this one included. I have had the incredible privilege of living between the worlds, in the sense that I have actually spent a substantial amount of time in my life with people who were not physical in the way that we know the physical. I have learned from them, and loved them and feared them and tasted of them. I know that there is a soul because I experienced complete release from the boundaries of my body. It has been my great privilege to personally experience these things, and so it is my duty to tell you this: I believe not only from faith, but from actual experience, that what I have written of is true.

Over our history, we have rejected what is actually the greater part of reality by labeling it as "supernatural." Most of us believe—or fear in our hearts—that the soul is not real, and that there is no world beyond this one. We die into a question, or into that flickering and inadequate medium that we call "faith."

My visitor would agree with the skeptics in one key way: there is no supernatural. But his explanation of the

way parts of reality that we have labeled supernatural actually work offers a promise for the future that is truly
breathtaking. He has opened the door to the proverbial
undiscovered country, and invited us in. For it becomes
very clear, from what he says, that there exists a powerful
science of the soul that we can master just as certainly as
we have mastered the science of the atom.

We have hidden from this science, and pretended to
ourselves that it doesn't exist. We have done this in order
to isolate ourselves from the overwhelming power of the
world that lies beyond.

He has left us with a challenge and a promise: it is time
for us to face the reality of this other world, and to come
to terms with the fact that we can detect it, communicate with it, and see beyond the curtain of denial and lies
that now obscures our vision of it.

In the end, I thought perhaps he was a dead man, come
in fulfillment of prophecy in this perilous age. If so, then
he is a herald, for what he said will lead to a revolution in
our understanding of ourselves and the universe around
us. We are about to make a discovery of fundamental importance: not only is the world of the soul real, it is accessible to verifiable scientific exploration. In fact, scientific
method would be essential to success in the effort to
identify the soul. Science—our science as we understand
it now—can part the curtain between the living and the

dead. We can thus come into real relationship with an ancient world that is much larger than this one, that is so much our true home that we have never left it, but only retreated into this small corner of it that we call the universe. He has challenged us to drop the pretense and face what we truly are, creatures who have always had the capacity to walk in the electric paths of heaven—but only if we dare. Only if we dare.

WHO WAS HE?

When I woke up the next morning and went out into the crowded lobby of the hotel, I was struck a blow by each face that I saw. At the breakfast tables and at the hotel desk, they were all crying out, "I'm alone and I'm dying," and I knew in every cell of my being what he had meant—what he had *really* meant—when he said that this is a fallen world. I knew also, with a certainty that will never, ever leave me, that he was not fallen. I had been with somebody who had never tasted the mystery of our isolation, but who understood the loneliness of mankind better than we do.

As I walked through that hotel lobby, there was a fire burning in me. I saw that what feels like a hopeless, immutable reality—that we are fallen—is itself just another illusion. All that lies between us and the ascension of which he spoke is exactly nothing. We can ascend right now, immediately, all of us.

I was off to the airport after a couple of last stops at
bookstores. I felt very strange, as if the world around me
was not quite real. People talked, I talked, I signed books.
But it was all happening somewhere far away, each present moment seeming as if it was a memory.

I remembered the night's events with perfect clarity.
There was no question in my mind but that it had all been
real. I knew, though, that it had been a very strange experience, and I suspected that on some deeper level I was
reacting to it much as I had to my close encounters. This
was why I called my wife and told her never to let me
forget that the encounter had been real. If something
happens to you that is sufficiently strange, it soon comes
to seem curiously illusive. Before too long, the brain files
it in the realm of dreams, even though it was real.

It was a Saturday morning, and the publicist from the
publishing house only stayed with me for a short time. I
did not know quite how to approach her about what had
happened, so I said nothing. A few weeks later, I would
call her and describe my visitor to her. She would tell me
that she had never seen such a man, as would a number of
other people I knew in Toronto. But that would not be
the end of it, not entirely. I would go down some strange
paths in search of this man.

When I got settled in the plane, I had a chance to reflect. I watched the world of the north slip away beneath

me. Gone were the days that I would be returning to New York. We were now living more-or-less in exile, due to harassment and subtle threats from shadowy parties. There had been many financial reverses, much hardship. I had lost my beloved cabin in the woods in upstate New York. With it had gone most of my close encounter experiences. But now I had this. At least I had this.

I felt a familiar sense of self-assurance. How could I ever forget a word of that incredible conversation? And anyway, I had my notes. But I knew that this was all an illusion. Had I not also had a number of ultra-strange experiences, I might have soon lost a great deal of what had been said. But I knew remembering it correctly would be hard. I estimated that it would take me six months or so to transcribe the conversation and get it into order. I never dreamed how hard it would actually be. It took me years to get this put together in a manner that even begins to do justice to the original conversation.

As I flew home, I wondered who he had been. I wondered about the might-have-beens. What might have happened if I'd attacked him and tied him up and called the police? Or if I hadn't drunk the white liquid and had instead followed him? Or if I'd had a camera with me and taken a picture?

Who was he?

When I got back to San Antonio, I set about writing

down the conversation. Immediately, I ran into trouble. These huge ideas, and new ideas, were even more elusive than I'd thought they would be. I had them in my mind, most certainly, but when I tried to transfer them to paper they became . . . well, me. Where was the soaring sense of newness and assurance that had been there when we were face-to-face? Where was the excitement?

I struggled for days. But it all came out sounding like a mix of warmed over Catholicism and new-age mysticism. Me, very definitely . . . and not even me at my best.

I began to think that I needed another session with this man. I needed to know him, actually, to get his direct participation in the writing process. Until you lose track of somebody, it seems so easy to find them. But, in this world, if you don't have a name or an address or at least a neighborhood, you're in trouble.

I hadn't tried harder to get him to identify himself because he had seemed so familiar to me at the time. Why would I want my grandfather to tell me his name, or my uncle to give me his address? When I was with him, I might even have been able to say his name. It had seemed as if I'd known him all my life.

Which got me to thinking. Maybe I had known him. Maybe, in fact, he'd been in Texas when I was a child. So perhaps it would be interesting to ask around in San Antonio. What I did was to tell people the story of the meet-

ing. I didn't pick and choose. I simply told anybody who
seemed interested. And then I would ask them if they'd
ever seen this person. I described him as a relatively slight
man somewhere between sixty-five and eighty, with a
dusting of white hair and a sharply-featured but kind face.
I did not think that anybody who had met him would
ever forget him.

For the most part, I drew a blank. Then one friend
had a rather interesting reaction. He thought perhaps he
had met this man, or somebody quite like him, back in the
sixties.

He had been a student of percussion at the time, and
his teacher was a percussionist with the Houston Symphony. The percussionist was a shy man, preferring his
own company to the point that nobody had ever entered
his apartment. He often wore gloves, and would clean his
hands frequently. He took a liking to my friend, who was
amazed one day to be invited to his apartment.

There were books everywhere, in bookcases lining
every wall. While his teacher was out of the room, he
looked at some of these books. They seemed concentrated on two subjects: UFOs and radar. My friend was
confused. He had expected books on musical subjects, because his teacher was not just any percussionist. He was
thought to be one of the great percussionists in the world.
But here he was, obviously obsessed with what, in the six-

ties, was a very odd subject indeed—UFOs. And radar? A percussionist?

They completed their time together, and my friend did not see his teacher for some days. Then shocking news came. The apartment had burned. The fire had been so hot that it had actually burned all the books to ash. Houston fire department officials were doubly mystified. Not only had this fire been hot enough to burn closed books, which require high heat to be completely incinerated if the pages aren't exposed to air, there had been almost no damage to other apartments in the building. Even stranger, the percussionist had disappeared and there were no human remains of any kind found in the apartment.

He has never been seen since. But he did leave my friend, who has become a prominent composer, a wonderful legacy: his love of percussion, which is central to his work.

The facial descriptions of the two men were not close enough to be an exact match, but I really did wonder, as I still do, whether or not they were the same person.

In the days when we had our cabin in upstate New York, the children used to see a man in black clothing moving through the woods, or standing at a distance and watching them. His presence made me and my wife extremely nervous, and I used to try to see him myself, but I never did. I really wondered—hoped, perhaps—that he was just an imaginary playmate.

Then, one day, the foreman of a group of men who were clearing some poison ivy from the trees along our driveway appeared at the house. They were not finished but they were quitting. They didn't want any money, they just wanted to get out of there. The reason was that they had seen an alien cross the driveway not twenty feet from where they were working. They described him as human-looking, wearing black clothes, but with a face "like an animal" and "glaring" eyes.

I could understand their desire to leave. My reputation in the area was already so notorious because of odd events being witnessed around my place, that I was afraid that I'd reach a point that nobody would work for me.

After that, the children often saw the man, even when my son was in his teens. He brought some kids down from Andover for a weekend. We had strict instructions from him not to discuss aliens, UFOs or anything like that. My teenager's opinion, at that point, was that I actually *was* the most embarrassing father in the world.

The kids slept out in the woods. I told my son that this was foolish, because the visitors would be bound to be interested. He said that they wouldn't be bothered. By that time, the ultra-high-level strangeness of his childhood encounters had made them seem so dreamlike to him that he was eager and willing to dismiss them as fantasies.

I had no problem with that. I had done it many times myself. However, his friends had an active night. They saw seven balls of light floating through the woods. Just at dawn, one of them saw a swarm of gnats turn into the face of a woman—a phenomenon I had observed myself once or twice, but which I had never reported because it was just too strange. And they had also seen, standing off in the woods, a man in tight-fitting black clothing, a man that Andrew recalled from his childhood.

They had quite a bit of fun, actually, and Andrew actually told them some of his childhood stories, which are among the most marvelous encounter experiences I have ever heard . . . when he remembers them . . . when he will speak about them.

That was the last time we saw the man of the woods. As I have never laid eyes on him, I cannot be certain that he was the same person whom I met in Toronto. Whether he had glaring eyes or an animal-like face or not, he never hurt anybody. The foreman said that he looked "ratlike," and the man in Toronto did have rather sharp features. But not that sharp. Of course, somebody who's frightened tends to exaggerate.

I explored one other possibility. In his marvelous book

The Labyrinth of the Grail, Masonic author William Mann discusses the legend that some Knights Templar refugees from Europe made it to Canada after the order was destroyed by the French king and the church, arriving in 1398.

The Templars were probably the single most important secret order ever founded. They apparently found ancient secrets in Jerusalem that eventually came to form the core of Masonic teaching about the value of man and the meaning of human freedom. The United States is founded upon these principles. It is a Masonic project, and thus the Templar heritage is of fundamental importance to the institutional structure of the world's most successful republic.

There is a text now known as The Zeno Narrative that historian Frederick Pohl has claimed indicates that Prince Henry Sinclair, a Templar leader, arrived in Nova Scotia in June of 1398. Among the Micmac Indians who are native to the area, there are still legends of Glooscap, who tirelessly explored the countryside. There is a possibility that there was a survival from Henry Sinclair's expedition— people who preserved their cultural tradition and secret knowledge even into modern times? My visitor described himself in many ways, and interestingly one of them was that he was "a Canadian" who didn't pay taxes and didn't have a driver's license.

Canadian friends have pointed out that it's exceptionally hard to escape taxes there. One way it could be done, though, would be if you had been in Canada before the arrival of the French and the English, and had made a point of never joining the state.

So maybe he was a representative of a Templar survival that still persists in Canada.

It is here that my trail ends. I was never able to find out anything more definite about him. He could have been an alien, or one of the human beings he mentioned who live off planet, or an angel, or even an image of God. He could also have been a very brilliant and thus also very clever fan of my books, who succeeded at three in the morning at throwing me enough off-balance that I was susceptible to the subtle messages and suggestions that he sent.

It would have been fabulously interesting to be able to come to a final conclusion about who this man was. I think it is obvious to anybody who reads the words of the Master of the Key that he is in possession of remarkable knowledge. I also suspect, however, that this master of subtlety and ambiguity wanted to be seen as holographically as he sees God. At times, I felt like I was talking to an ordinary person. At other moments, he seemed to have the powerful and joyous presence of an angel. When he uttered the words "cruel to God," there came into my heart the feeling that this *was* God. There was a note of sorrow in the tone so gentle and yet so great, that it was easy for me to feel, in that moment, that the great God of the universe was sitting right there expressing a deeply personal and yet unimaginably vast pain.

He inspired me very powerfully. Like my friend the composer, the rest of my life is going to revolve around my time with him. The deepest part of me resonates with a kind of assurance that this man possessed the truth and told the truth. Beneath the questions that he left unanswered there is a kind of bedrock of certainty that they are good and true questions. Beneath the information, there is the same sense of truth.

If the Master of the Key did tell the truth, then he pointed the way to our becoming an entirely different species. In this sense, his words are an engine of evolution. They are a light in the blind darkness of our world, out of which we can conceivably forge a whole new mankind.

The

PROPHECY

of the KEY

The Key seems to me to be all but unique in the way it breaks down the barrier between science and religion, man and machine, human and God. It suggests a new vision of each of us as a full and complete repository of God. It suggests, quite incredibly, how science can become a form of prayer: an instrument through which we can clearly and objectively address the higher world.

The process of evolution is not automatic. Far from it. We are expected to take an active role in personal transformation, in social transformation and even in the transformation of intelligence itself, through the creation of machines more intelligent than ourselves, machines that will ultimately become conscious. One of the most haunting moments in the conversation comes when I ask the Master if he is a conscious machine. He replies, "If I was, I would deceive you."

If such a machine comes into being in the future and

gains access to movement through time, then perhaps he can best be understood as an artifact of its own process of self-creation.

Whether the Master is a man or a machine, the conversation also points to a fundamentally new way to find union with God. For thousands of years, we have been searching for God on paths that are essentially exterior to us. We have been disciplining ourselves as monks, enduring privations, wandering the world in search of enlightenment.

The Master suggests a different road. He does not offer an outer path, but subtly suggests that we allow the flux of life to carry us where it will, as we seek light within ourselves. And not just a small bit of it. He asserts that we are not mere fragments, like "crumbs in a cake," but that each of us really does contain the entire Kingdom of God, even to the extent that we can come to know the whole of creation as God knows it. There is the implication that something has changed about mankind over the past two thousand years, and that we are now more able to experience this than we were then.

When you say God, you think of somebody outside of yourself. You think as the age of worship thinks. Over the last age, that of Pisces, the elemental body was changed by this process of worship. It is not the

same as it was two thousand years ago. Now the receptacle is larger. Now each of you can contain all of the universe. That was not true then. Now this is a species of sacred beings. But you are babies, and so still ignorant of your powers. The last age was the age of the external God. This is the age of God within.

This quite surprising statement seems to infer that history has been a process of evolution, that we have been in some way changed by the passage of time. Other statements imply that a large-scale plan for mankind is in effect.

We measured the rate at which you would expand and grow very precisely, and fitted your development to a calendar which we devised called the Zodiac. In your writings, Whitley, you have wondered why mankind would have such a long-count calendar. Why were simple farmers in need of it? They were not. We needed it.

Who is this "we"? And why did they need a measure of the ages? When one examines history in the light of the Zodiac, some very curious hints emerge, especially in the Middle East, where the Zodiac seems to have been consciously used as a marker of the epochs.

I have discussed this both in *Confirmation* and in *The Coming Global Superstorm,* but it is worth repeating here that the Sphinx, which is a gigantic image of a lion, was sited so that the constellation of Leo rose directly over it in 10,500 B.C. It has also been found by geologists to be very much older than was previously thought—in fact, that it might date from that period. If so, then it must be a monument to the Age of Leo, which began at that time.

The Old Testament, which was written during the Age of Aries the Ram, contains more references to that animal than any other. Similarly, Christ was born just as the Age of Pisces began. He is called the Fisher of Men, and his apostles are fishermen. Indeed, Piscean imagery is so prevalent in the gospels that early Christians identified themselves with the symbol of the fish, which has been resuscitated by modern fundamentalists.

The parallels between the symbolic content of these ancient writings and monuments and the Zodiacal ages in which they took place cannot be an entire coincidence. It suggests a level of planning higher than any of which we are consciously aware, and it is my belief that the Master of the Key is a part of this level of planning. It is possible that he has deposited these words as an artifact for the age we are presently entering, which is Aquarius.

In this age, the water in which the fish has been so comfortably swimming will get poured out. Although this implies an increase in freedom, it also means that the medium in which we have been living will no longer be there to support us. This medium, of course, is the earth itself, and the Master of the Key warns about changes in the earth's environment that are going to place us in the position of either finding a way to expand off the planet or face possible extinction.

It was a statement of his about the nature of ice ages that inspired *The Coming Global Superstorm*:

Because air at the surface is getting warmer, the north polar ice is melting, reducing the salinity of the Laurentian sea. At some point, winds crossing this sea due to the increasing difference between lower and higher atmospheric pressures will warm the northern ocean so much that the temperature differential needed to pump the North Atlantic Current will not be sufficient, and the current will slow down, stop, or stop flowing so far north. This same mechanism always triggers ice ages, and would happen within a few thousand years no matter what. However, human activity has sped up the process of atmospheric warming, so the change will be sooner and stronger. The greater part of human industry and culture, along with the species' most educated populations, will be destroyed in a single season. This will happen

suddenly and without warning, or rather, the warning will not be recognized for what it is.

This statement turned out to be a very exact description of a process that has been discussed for some years within the paleoclimatological community as an explanation for climatic upheavals in the past, and we were able to actually use their findings in *Superstorm* to support our theory.

The one thing that their studies did not confirm was the storm itself. In "The Great Climate Flip-flop" by William H. Calvin in the *Atlantic Monthly* in January of 1998, it was postulated that the change had come very quickly in the past. Interestingly, the last abrupt change took place, according to James White, a University of Colorado climatologist, approximately 12,500 years ago, in 10,500 B.C., at the same time that the Sphinx was apparently built. (Although some Egyptologists continue to claim that the Sphinx is of more recent origin, the evidence of water erosion on the object is overwhelmingly convincing to geologists.)

The Sphinx reflects a fundamental principle that is echoed in the words of the Master of the Key in numerous places. The Sphinx has a lion's claws, a bull's body and the head of a man. In esoteric tradition, the riddle of the Sphinx has been this: What has the strength of the bull, the courage of the lion and the intelligence of the man? The answer is never quite clear, except to those who have achieved this balance. More plainly spoken, the idea of the triad as expressed in modern esoteric philosophy is this: that positive and negative forces, pressing against each other, come into balance. Buckminster Fuller called this the fundamental principle of the universe. The Master of the Key relates it most notably to his rather astonishing assertion that Buddhism, Christianity and Islam are actually a single religion.

> Christianity is the active side of the triad, Islam the passive, Buddhism the reconciling. Christianity seeks God, Islam surrenders to God, Buddhism finds God. When you see these as three separate systems, you miss the great teaching of which each contains but a part. Seek the kingdom as a Christian, give yourself to God as a Muslim, find your new companion in the dynamic silence of Buddhist meditation.

There seems to be a great truth in these words, which, like so much of this material, refer to a larger scale of things than we are used to thinking about. We think in terms of tens or perhaps hundreds of years, not thousands. And we certainly do not think on a scale so large that it would find a means of reconciling three great religions and practicing them as one.

Indeed, it is essential that the whole issue of scale be addressed in any commentary on the Key. For example, the Master's conception of God is at once much larger and infinitely more personal than our own. His model for deity is the hologram. God is not equally present in all things, but totally present in all things.

This idea does two things. It redefines not only man but every creature as something immense and incredibly important. But it also makes one feel rather frozen and helpless. How can I possibly become aware of a greatness like this, that is so far from my everyday life, even if it resides in every particle of my being?

He did not describe this change as a sort of flash of inner light that would instantly transform everything. Rather, he pointed in a totally new direction.

Conscious energy is not like unconscious energy, the servant of those who understand its laws. To gain access to the powers of conscious energy, you must evolve a relationship with it. Learn its needs, learn to fulfill them. But also remember, it is part of the electromagnetic spectrum, easily detectable by your science as it exists now. You can learn to signal and

> be heard, and to record response. The veil between
> the worlds can fall. The undiscovered country can
> become your backyard.

This is a truly gigantic promise that suggests the existence
of a new and entirely unexpected human frontier. When
he says "the veil between the worlds can fall," he means
the barrier between the living and the dead. This is made
clear by the reference to the "undiscovered country,"
which is an allusion to a famous speech of Hamlet's, from
Act II, Scene 3 of Shakespeare's play: "the dread of something after death, the undiscover'd country from whose
bourn no traveler returns . . ."

The Master of the Key had clear and intimate knowledge of the world of the dead. He spoke of the effects of
death on our history, for example, when he described how
the destruction of the European Jews had critically ham-
pered our scientific progress.

> The Holocaust reduced the intelligence of the human
> species by killing too many of its most intellectu-
> ally competent members. It is why you are still using
> jets seventy-five years after their invention. The un-
> derstanding of gravity is denied you because of the
> absence of the child of a murdered Jewish couple.

This child would have unlocked the secret of gravity.
But he was not born.

This was one of the most shocking statements I have ever heard in my life. It implies that a completely new moral order will emerge when we can see the real consequences of our actions. I thought to myself at the time: "We were not responsible for this. It was a result of historical forces beyond our control." He quickly agreed with that, saying that our present situation was not a punishment but simply an inevitable outcome of events.

But he also made stunning pleas for personal responsibility on a scale from which we usually distance ourselves. His pleas for the poor and the innocent stirred me to my depths. I will never forget for an instant:

> **Remember this: every one of you is entirely and completely responsible for the welfare of all others. So if a child is starving in Liberia, Whitley, you are personally and entirely responsible for him.**

It is beyond my power to communicate the resonance of his voice, or the richness of its emotional content. However, there was something about the assurance in these words—as if he innocently trusted me never to doubt them and to act on them always—that has filled my heart.

It has also left me with a huge question: What is to be done on behalf of the children? Should I become a pilgrim on their behalf?

> Go to Calcutta or Lagos or Bogotá and give yourself to the first street urchin you meet as his helper and lifelong servant. Do it without question or hesitation. You say that you want to worship God? Kneel to this little one and you kneel to God.

How those words haunt me. They have the ring of "come and follow me," but am I not like the rich man whose possessions prevented him from taking the greatest of all journeys?

> Remember the Eye of the Needle? A rich man may pass through the Eye of the Needle if he uses his wealth to enrich the world. Those who cling to their wealth are dying souls.

I have asked myself, "What is wealth?" I think that my wealth lies in two areas: my ability to write, and my incredible luck at having met, in the flesh, some very great and extraordinary beings, the most forthcoming of whom was certainly the Master of the Key. So my use of my wealth to enrich the world lies in creating books like this

one. However, when I retire, I can easily imagine myself
going somewhere deep in the third world and starting an
orphanage. Once, when passing through the streets of a
huge third-world city, I saw all the street children and
I thought to myself: "Each of them is as precious and potentially as valuable as our children at home." But we pretend, don't we, not only that they don't have as much
value, but that they aren't even there.

> The first world is a slave owner. You are all slave
> owners. You have enslaved the people of God, your
> own brothers and sisters who are poor. Do you un-
> derstand the cruelty of the world as it is now, with
> five billion people enslaved to a billion? Each of you
> owns five slaves. But you never see your slaves, so
> you need not be concerned about their health and
> welfare. You let them fend for themselves, locked
> away in their poverty and suffering. I will tell you
> this: when one of my children dies in the slave bar-
> rens that cover this planet, I also die, and you, my
> arrogant friend, even you die a little.

He identifies himself holographically—here, calling himself the parent of the poor of the world, a role claimed for
Christ. But in other places he implies different things. In
fact, through the course of the conversation he suggested

many identities for himself. Here are some of the ways he identified himself:

> My being includes all elements of the earth, and thus
> I am part of all bodies.

> I am human.

> I belong to many worlds.

> Christ said it: I am the son of man, meaning that
> Christ is all and all are Christ.

> So also, no matter what you may call me, I am in God.

> I'm only a Canadian.

> My home is within you.

When I asked him his name, he said, "What if I said Michael?" Then he suggested that maybe his name was Legion, the biblical demon. In the end, perhaps this was his most telling identification of himself:

> I can imagine no greater honor than to be called
> human.

But he did not characterize us as being fully human. He
explained matters this way:

> A true human being has four levels of mind. Most
> of you have only three, and perhaps a vestige of
> the fourth. Your destiny is to enter the humanity of
> the universe. But you may not fulfill it.

So the question became for me, What is this fourth level
of mind and how do we attain it? His answer to this
particular question goes to the heart of his uniqueness.
Instead of vague generalities, he made very specific statements that took the whole issue out of the mystical arena
and placed it firmly in a practical context.

> A part of the electromagnetic field that fills the ner-
> vous system rests a few centimeters above the skin,
> outside of the body. This field is an organ just like
> the heart or the brain. It is in quantum superposi-
> tion, the electrons effectively everywhere in the uni-
> verse and nowhere specific. It may be imprinted by
> information from anywhere and any time. With it,
> you may see other worlds, you may see the past and
> the future, you may see into the lives of those around
> you. You may haunt God.

What he may have meant by the cryptic sentence, "You may haunt God," I do not know. Perhaps we'll find that out when we are better able to utilize this electromagnetic organ of ours.

But the rest of the statement is richly informative. In fact, there has been considerable scientific research into this electromagnetic field and even into its possible properties as a medium for what we call "psychic" exchange. In their paper "Does Psi Exist?" published in the *Psychological Bulletin* (vol. 115, no. 1, 4–18) in 1994, Daryl Bem and Charles Honorton attempt a theory of psychic activity. They theorize that "Bell's theorem states that any model of reality that is compatible with quantum mechanisms must be nonlocal. It must allow for the possibility that results of observations at two arbitrarily distant locations can be correlated in ways that are incompatible with any physically permissible causal mechanism."

Could it be that the Master of the Key has identified a specific mechanism by which information gathered non-locally can be introduced into the brain and processed there? He mentions that the electromagnetic organ of which he speaks is centered in the pineal, the enigmatic gland that is known to produce melatonin in response to light levels, and which, in lower animals, contains minute amounts of magnetite, which some researchers believe that the human pineal may also contain. Most notably, the pineal has been found to be the source of *N,N*-dimethyltryptamine, or DMT, an extremely powerful but short-acting psychedelic.

In his book *DMT: The Spirit Molecule* (Park Street Press, 2001), Dr. Rick Strassman explains that high DMT doses can induce every sort of spiritual experience. In 1990, Dr. Strassman commenced the first new research on the effects of psychedelics to be conducted in the United States in twenty years. He administered four hundred doses of DMT to sixty volunteers over a five-year period at the University of New Mexico's School of Medicine in Albuquerque. He chronicled the experiences of his volunteers, commenting from his observations that "we enter into invisible realms, ones we cannot normally sense and whose presence we can scarcely imagine. Even more surprising, these realms appear to be inhabited."

Dr. Strassman's research has challenged the assumption that stimulation of the pineal results in mere hallucinations. "Our volunteers' reports were so clear, convincing and 'real' that I repeatedly thought, This sounds like nothing I've ever heard about in my therapy patients' dream life. It is much more bizarre, well-remembered and internally consistent."

Additionally, there were consistencies among the observations made by different volunteers that suggested that they were seeing as if through a window into another world, rather than generating random hallucinations.

In ancient times, the pineal was thought of as the "third eye," and the Master of the Key suggested that its vision depended upon the electromagnetic field around the body remaining "nonlocal" even as it gathered impressions. The gland is actually a vestigial eye in some lower invertebrates.

The Master of the Key is very specific about how to access information through this mechanism, explaining in precise terms why a familiar meditative state would be necessary to succeed with the process. Robert Monroe, in his classic *Journeys Out of the Body*, describes it as an asleep/ awake state, "body sleeping, mind awake," and the Monroe Institute offers tapes that guide the user in how to achieve it. Additionally, in the Gurdjieff Foundation, I was taught about a state of meditation where one concentrates one's attention on physical sensation and allows the automatic "inner talking" of the mind to proceed on its own. In the Gurdjieff discipline, this state of being objectively aware of oneself is the beginning of becoming truly awake.

It is a state that is described in one way or another in every meditative practice. What is new here is the why of the thing—that there would be an actual organ involved, and that this organ would need a higher form of attention to function. What makes the author of these words a master is the clarity and simplicity of his explanations of what until now have been complete mysteries.

I cannot say that this particular part of his teaching surprised me, as I had been meditating regularly for twenty-eight years when I had my conversation with him. Often, I have experienced a bright light inside my head while in a meditative state. It is an intense, uniform white glow with cathedral depth to it, but when one really tries to look at it, it disappears. If, however, a balance can be maintained between seeing and not seeing, much can be gained.

I cannot say with certainty that I have seen other worlds using this means, but I have certainly glimpsed some wondrous sights. For example, I've observed street scenes so detailed and rich that it is hard not to think that they were real. However, I cannot point to somebody else who had precisely the same vision, and certainly not under anything approaching controlled conditions.

Once I asked to see a world slightly worse off than our own, and another slightly better off. The one that was worse off was divided between two dictatorial states, as if Hitler had defeated the west and not attacked Russia.

I only saw a few brief glimpses of this ramshackle, pol-
luted place, and they were so strange that I initially could
not understand the meaning of what I was looking at. It
was only the movement of things like bodies and vehi-
cles that enabled me to integrate the vision in such a way
that I could begin to tell that I was looking at a wide
avenue in a city. The buildings were long and almost
featureless. A vehicle—a bus?—passed. It was filled with
dark-eyed, spindly creatures. The sky was brown with
pollution, worse than the worst Mexico City or Houston
has to offer.

A few days later, on October 13, 1996, the entire place
abruptly exploded in a massive nuclear war of the kind
we never had. The two totalitarian states had not been
able to maintain the same kind of balance that the flexible, innovative west had maintained with the suspicious,
aggressive Soviet Union. The total lack of freedom in this
world had destroyed it.

The Master of the Key is very clear about what happens
when a planet is destroyed. He explains exactly how we
are bound to our planet, and how the continued growth
of each soul is dependent upon the planet still being there.
But the planet I saw is now no longer habitable. So what
is happening to them now? The same thing that will happen to us if earth is destroyed:

We wait until and if the earth spins elemental bodies once again that fit all the attachments of our energetic bodies. If it does not, then we wait forever. We remain incomplete.

And if that doesn't happen, then we will miss our chance at ecstasy, and he makes it clear that this is a terrible thing indeed.

Energetic bodies hunger to be radiant. They taste of ecstasy and want desperately to find their way to the completion of joy. But energetic bodies need return to time to reconstruct what of themselves impedes their ecstasy. If they cannot, they must suffer the anguish of regret and the pain of being able to see, but not enter, joy. When you taste of ecstasy, your hunger for more is appalling. It is *appalling*. It has driven me to wander the world, to construct this shell of flesh, to seek you out and come to you with my message, to serve you, little child, as my master.

This last statement—"it has driven me to wander the world"—conceals some implications that were undoubtedly intended to disturb me. In 1 Peter, 5:8, the devil is described as "going about seeking whom he may devour."

And in the Catholic tradition, he is described as the one who "wanders the world, seeking the ruin of souls." But also, the seeker may wander the world in search of enlightenment, and he told me that I would find it by serving a little child. What this means, I think, is that he seeks to serve me, but also there is a warning implied, that if I misuse his wisdom, he will become something very different from what he at first appeared.

He has an entirely different view of evil than what has been in the past. It isn't the biblical view or the modern, mechanistic view, or even the awful view that evil is something we bring on ourselves. But rather, he doesn't see it as something to be avoided, so much as to be understood and used. He puts it this way:

> **The darkness is the compassion of God, which gives us our vision of the universe. So also, the darkness in your heart is your own compassion toward yourself, for unless you bore evil, you would not be able to discern good.**

This remarkable statement offers a whole new approach to evil, viewing it as a tool rather than some awful, external force that can only victimize us. Like the whole of the Key, it demands personal responsibility not just for one's own acts but for the whole world.

The Master's definition of evil is strikingly simple and new:

Entropy is the natural tendency of all things to disintegrate. Evil is the addition of intention to that process.

He also suggests that evil is a necessity in human life, "without which you would not be able to discern good."

However, this is also a brilliantly satanic defense of evil, and the dark side of the Master cannot be ignored. However, he spoke so eloquently of compassion that it is hard to see how he could be essentially evil.

The second of the two worlds that I saw was different from ours in another way than the first. The creatures in it were not even close to us in the way they looked. But the one I saw, who also saw me, had a lot of expression in his or her face that I could identify with. The expression was one of rueful compassion. They'd had a hard history. But their world had recently changed in a fundamental way. They had survived a terrible environmental crisis— had come through fire, as it were.

Now theirs was a culture based not on punishment and retribution, but on what the Master defines as compassion—"finding what others need the most and giving it to them."

They were just a little bit ahead of where we are now, in the process of coming to the end of the culture of blame and seeking in the dark for some sort of a better way.

The transformation of our world into a place of compassion is at the core of the Key. Compassion would appear to be the essential ingredient in forming a completely new kind of society. But it is not obvious that the conventional definition of compassion—that it is a sort of vague acceptance of the ill will and mistakes of others—will work. Instead, the Master demands a much more rigorous sort of compassion. This compassion is not passive at all. It proactively seeks what others need the most and gives it to them. The personal morality he advocates—"each of you is entirely responsible for all the others"—translates into a beautiful vision of a whole new social order.

In such a world, it is everybody's duty and delight to find what every other they come into contact with needs most from them, and give it to them.

The operative word is "delight." There is extraordinary joy involved in living like this. Putting on the chains of judgment and blame is an amazing feeling. And it isn't as if one must give gold to the thief. Rather give him what will raise him from his habit of thievery.

In a compassionate world, for example, there might

well be prisons. They would not be places of punishment, however, but rather places where the congenitally dangerous were kept in the interest of safety, and the mistaken were restored to social usefulness. It would be a world where we could tell the difference between the helplessly criminal and the reformable, because we would have applied clear-eyed science to the problem instead of approaching criminality through the filter of our various agendas.

A compassionate world would be very, very different from this one. It would be less a fallen world. It would be a happier world. And it can certainly be afforded. As the Master makes clear, the culture of blame is costly, and always leads to the eventual destruction of the unbalanced societies that are based in it.

In our conversation, the Master at one point described prayer in a completely amazing way. He said that it was "a lost science of communication." Throughout our conversation, he alluded to an earlier civilization that seemed to have some powers greater than our own. In this particular area, it must have truly excelled, for he describes it as having built a subtle machine that girded the world and was used as a means of communication between man and God.

I have often wondered whether or not the legends of

lost civilizations were some kind of inner myth about a thread we have dropped on the way toward objective understanding of the world—that the golden age they suggest is actually in the future, not the past.

But I no longer think this. There are simply too many strange ruins around the world to dismiss the possibility that an advanced civilization once existed here, and now is gone. I think that we may not even be at the pinnacle of our history, but rather on the long, declining slope of it.

The Master tells a wonderful story, which he describes as "Hindu," about God entering a pig and becoming so involved in its material delights that he forgets that he is the creator of the universe. He says that we are the spirit in the pig, and that he is here, among others, to awaken us by killing the pig.

At one point, he implies that he and his kind are actually working *against* our discovering our situation, in order to force us to act on our own behalf. And this seems to be one of the essential subtleties of the Key—that we must take action on our own behalf. In a sense, what is happening to us now is very like a birth experience. The comfortable womb of the earth is about to become untenable for us. We will not be able to live here much longer with anything like the comfort we have enjoyed thus far. The water of Aquarius is indeed being poured out, and the little fish that has been growing and evolving in it is going to face the seemingly impossible situation of needing to live out of water.

Perhaps the Master's most interesting claim is that there is conscious energy, and that it is part of the energetic spectrum that we can already detect. If this is true, then there is a whole new world right at hand that is simply waiting for us to begin communication with it. This is an explosive concept, especially given that there has been some scientific work that suggests that it may be true.

The original studies were carried out by Dr. William Roll with the support of the Mind Science Foundation. An attempt was made to determine whether or not objective science could detect anything in areas where hauntings were commonly reported.

Instruments detected the presence of unusual electromagnetic plasmas and areas of markedly reduced air temperature in some of these locations with a consistency that made it possible to conclude that an anomalous phenomenon was being consistently observed in areas where ghosts were seen.

According to the *New Scientist*: "Of the emerging evidence, the most convincing is of sharply fluctuating magnetic fields at spots where ghosts appear."

It is becoming easy to detect these fields, even for amateurs, and the presence of orbs of light in the area of hauntings is beginning to be observed on videotape, as well as brief snatches of vocalization on both audio- and videotape.

In addition, physicist Frank Tipler, while devising a mathematical model of the end of the universe, found that he had stumbled upon a proof of the existence of God. The book he wrote about this, *The Physics of Immortality*, has had a quietly powerful effect within the scientific community, as other physicists and mathematicians have glimpsed the shadow of a living presence within the structures of nature.

The Master was completely at ease with this idea, speaking as if he could see not only with the eyes of the living, but also with the eyes of the dead. He was a wise and deeply humorous man. His emotions were gently powerful. When we talked about sin, in such a very, very different way from before, I felt that I was face-to-face with somebody who had experienced the disappointments that surround it personally. When he commented that sin is "cruel to God," I saw for an instant the enormous—and, I suspect, true—scale of human life.

The irony is that, isolated on this little dust mote of a planet lost in the far away, there really is a race of extraordinary beings struggling to face their eternal lives, and to find their place in the consciousness of God.

I do not know if I will ever meet the Master of the Key

again. I hope so. Sometimes, I remember things that I did not put in this book—not because they were intentionally withheld, but because I cannot recall them in enough detail to write them down. For example, afterward I mentioned to my wife that he had told me the day of my death. I don't remember that now. There were also other things said that perhaps were not spoken so much as communicated through the flood of love that seemed to pour off this man. I can only say that, whoever he was, he loved us in the most amazingly intimate, informed and joyous way that it is possible to imagine.

As time passes, I suspect that the scientific information that he presented is going to be verified. For example, he made a passing reference to nitrous oxide as a medium for powerful computers. To my surprise, I found what was almost certainly a reference to this idea in the October 3, 1998, issue of the New Scientist. It seems that the gas nitric oxide might theoretically make a powerful medium for a whole new kind of computer, one immeasurably more powerful than what we have now. Not only that, the brain already uses nitric oxide in its own functioning, something that I certainly did not know before having this conversation.

I have been working on this book for years. I have tried my best to convey the words of the Master of the Key as they were spoken to me. How well I have succeeded, I do not and cannot know. But reading his magnificent and wise sentences, I think that I have come as close as I could, short of being able to make a tape recording.

If there is anything that the Master said that I feel is most essential, it is probably the way he described our relationship to the earth. Our dysfunction, our profound disconnect—our being "fallen," as he put it—seems to stem from the central reality of this relationship.

So the eternal joy of humankind depends upon the health of the earth?
Completely.

We think of ourselves as individuals. My sins are my own. My neighbor's sins are his problem.
Every joy, every sorrow, every good, every evil belongs to all. All are responsible for all. All are dependent upon all. Humanity is one.

If we could take just those few lines as deep into each of our hearts as anything can go, we could find a motive to remake our world that is greater than the fearsome greed that now rules. We are in the process of being born as children of the earth, struggling to leave the planet and become in some way eternal. But we cannot do it by ignoring our planet's welfare and killing her.

Unless we find a place for ourselves in the universe that makes room for her to grow and heal the injuries she has sustained during the struggle of our birth, we are going to experience appalling trials. If earth dies, so do we. But if earth is flooded with new life, then so will we be.

I was at mass on the morning of November 19, 2000, when one of the readings chilled me to my very core. The words did more than amaze me, they almost left me breathless. I grew physically cold; in a certain sense, they horrified me.

I dropped the missal and stared ahead, barely hearing the mass that was now proceeding without one of the participants.

What I had read appeared to be a direct prophecy about this time, and about the Master of the Key. But how could I be involved in such a thing? It was crazy. I don't belong doing this. At most, I'm a minor writer, hardly even a comma on the page of literature. And yet here was this prophecy, and it seemed to be about the Master and, above all, about the essence of his warning and the essence of his message.

On that night, he had called himself "Michael." He had prophesied a terrible future, and told me enough about it to enable me to write a book of warning that was based in solid science. And here, in the book of Daniel, was another version of that same exact warning.

But more important, here were the radiant beings he talked about with such clarity and eloquence. Attaining this radiance is the aim of human life, very clearly. It was true for Daniel's time, and it would appear to be equally true now.

Here are the verses that I read that so awed me:

And at that time shall Michael stand up, the great prince which standeth for the children of thy people: and there shall be a time of trouble, such as was never seen since there was a nation even to that same time: and at that time thy people shall be delivered, every one that shall be found written in the book.

And many of them that sleep in the dust of the earth shall awake, some to everlasting life, and some to shame and everlasting contempt.

And they that be wise shall shine as the brightness of the firmament; and they that turn many to righteousness, as the stars for ever and ever.

—DANIEL 12: 1–3

The verses could not be more clear. It is the message of the Master. In the older translations like the King James Version I have quoted, Michael is referred to simply as "the great prince." The Revised Standard Version calls him "the captain of the angels," and Young's Literal calls him "the great head." (Robert Young published his translation in 1898. In it he attempts to preserve the original Greek and Hebrew tenses, structures and words as far as possible.)

I was left with this thought: we do not really know how to describe these great beings like Michael, through whom God shines. We call them angels, lords, princes, but how they may live from day to day, and what they may mean to themselves in the spirit is not given to us to know.

It also states in Daniel 12 that "the wicked will never understand," which saddens me greatly. When you read the words of the Master of the Key, you see with new eyes the real effect of sin, and you taste a little of the shining ecstasy that is the true aim of humankind.

I am a despised and discredited man. Most of this culture rejects me and calls me a liar. But I am a good man, and for whatever crazy reason, I have ended up with a book of very real wisdom that I think comes from somewhere close to the hand of God. So be it.

Why would a little nobody get this? Probably because the grand are too grand to listen to the words of an old man who knocks on their door in the middle of the night. He came to a nobody because only a nobody would let him in. I can only hope that his words will be heard . . . at

least by other nobodies. Maybe the great have their re-
ward already, in the wealth they share and the praise they
heap on each other's heads . . . perhaps like coals.

Later in chapter 12 of Daniel, in verse 5, it states: "Thou,
O Daniel, shut up the words, and seal the book, even to
the time of the end: many shall run to and fro, and knowledge shall be increased."

There could be no more perfect description of our
age. We race around like ants, in a world that is exploding
with knowledge.

But that was not the end of this phenomenal prophecy,
which I believe is a *very exact* description of events that are
happening right now. In 12:9 God says to Daniel, "the
words are closed up to the end of time."

Maybe the words have just been opened, and perhaps
that's why this ended up getting published at the real beginning of the new millennium, which is 2001.

If so, then it is time for the baby to open its eyes and
look around. The end of time is just the beginning of the
human journey. Let it be into the radiance that is God's
promise to Daniel and the hope of Michael's words.

Every heart which truly becomes one with the rest of
humanity, then will shine "as the stars forever and ever."

Whitley Strieber is the internationally best-selling author of more than twenty novels and works of nonfiction, among them the landmark work *Communion*, his account of a close encounter of the third kind that took place in December of 1985. He is also author of *The Wolfen, The Hunger* and *The Coming Global Superstorm*, all of which were made into feature films, most recently *Superstorm* as *The Day After Tomorrow*. He lives in California.

Visit his website at: www.UnknownCountry.com.